For my wondeful friend, Lindsey. Thank you for all your LOVE & support. ♡ libier

THROUGH THE WILDERNESS

WILDERNESS

A JOURNEY TO FREEDOM

LIBIER REYNOLDS

Scripture is taken from the HOLY BIBLE Most taken from the New International Version

Mollie Turbeville - Editor
Samantha Davalos - Book layout and design
Samantha Davalos - Book cover design
Haley Titus - Watercolor Artwork

LIBIER.COM

ISBN-13:
978-1986330671

ISBN-10:
1986330672
Your book has been assigned a CreateSpace ISBN.

DEDICATION

This book is dedicated to my husband Doug and my little girls Madelyn and
Haylee.
Without your love and encouragement this book would not exist.

ACKNOWLEDGMENTS

To the amazing people that believed in me by giving of their firstfruits to my cause! Thank you Roxy, Reyna and the Better Homes & Garden team! You have sowed into my dreams and life mission to share my story and I am forever grateful and you choose the perk to be inside of the book! I honor your name and your giving kindness. To all the other backers of my indiegogo campaign! You have also been incredibly uplifting helping me to believe in my book when I felt scared to launch your act of kindness toward me propelled me into action even when the amount of money we were raising didn't make the cut, I knew there was a reason why and decided to move forward because of your support! I thank you with all of my heart and look forward into hearing how God will bless your giving!

Doug, I want to thank you for countless hours of listening to me. I want to thank you for every prayer you prayed over me over our whole time healing and moving from the wilderness into our promised land. Honey, I am so incredibly grateful you are in my life. You are an amazing husband because you are real, honest and true. You've always been so quick to ask for forgiveness and to look within to make the changes. I love you and I am so grateful that we get to do life together. Thank you for always encouraging me to do my best and for always reassuring me that I was enough just as I was. Thank you for your help with the girls when I just had no strength. Thank you for your forgiveness for my rude behavior. Thank you for the love that you've chosen to put into **ac-**

tion as we've walked this difficult road. I feel so grateful and blessed that I get to call you my husband. I appreciate you and I love you and I am so happy that we've chosen to be obedient to God and his call for our lives! Thank you for your love, Doug. Thank you for your example of putting God first! I love you!

Girls. Mommy loves you so much and I am so grateful for your lives that have encouraged my healing and life! I will always love you and I will always be here for you. May God bless you through your whole lives to know yourselves as he knows you, beloved and cherished. Thank you for your tender forgiveness when mommy lost her self-control with you. Thank you for the wisdom you spoke to me even as a little human! Thank you for your genuine and pure love that has propelled me into my best life! You both are amazing in your own ways and I am so grateful I get to be your mother. I will never be perfect but I believe God made no mistake in pairing us together. May you know how much you mean to me and may you read my story with love and compassion. I love you!

To my family and friends. You've been such an important part of my life. Thank each and everyone of you for loving me, praying for me, talking with me and listening to me in my walk to healing. I love you so much and I am grateful God put you in my life!

CONTENTS

BROKEN

At a very young age, I was exposed to pornography. It shaped me, enslaved me in a cage of fear, anger, and bitterness. It marked my innocence. Robbed by the horrific images my little eyes saw unwillingly. Marked as dirty and shameful. I didn't understand at such a young age what my body was experiencing. It was deeply corrosive to my soul. I know that people who make pornography or people who take photos in lustful and seductive ways must hurt deeply. I believe not one person desires to be sexually explicit without experiencing extreme pain in their heart, from previous trauma. Back then when it happened to me, pornography wasn't as easily accessible. Now you scroll through social media, and even when you are not looking for it, an inappropriate photograph can mark the life of a little one in an instant. We are called to be different. Let's draw a line in the sand that stands for purity. Let's be the generation that says, "No more." It starts with you and me.

Before I could read a book, I was sexually abused by a few people. Eventually, I learned to read. My father was lost in alcoholism. At age six I just wanted a Cabbage Patch doll, you know the ones that smelled so good and you could just squeeze them and pretend they were your baby? I saw domestic violence in my home. My father left us to go to America. I didn't get that doll, I guess at that time more important things were happening. We had to move from our home to a different city in Mexico then to the U.S.A. I moved from wanting a doll to craving attention. Anyone's attention. At age 13 I had sex. Now I'm painfully aware it was statutory rape. I always dated someone way older than me. I had an abortion at eighteen, right before I graduated high school. Then again in my early twenties. At twenty-one, my mother tried to commit suicide. The doctors said she'd never wake up. Two years later, she attempted suicide again. The same thing, she woke up. The doctors couldn't believe it when she woke up. I moved to New York and then Los Angeles to follow my dreams of being an actress. After a few weeks of living in Los Angeles, I was raped. I slept in my car that night and drove back to Sacramento the next day, devastated. Done with my dreams.

In between all of this, I struggled with my image. I had extremely low self-esteem. At this time, I had no recollection of my sexual abuse. I had suppressed it into my thirties. I remember always feeling off. As if I were dirty. Shame was my friend. I would get so angry, sad, and confused and I would cut my arms to relieve myself of the pain I felt inside. I struggled with bulimia; I was always trying to find a guy to love me and give me worth. I had major control issues. Major trust issues. Major issues, period.

Have you ever found yourself in a wilderness of your own? I believe we all, at one time or another, question everything about who we are. Often the question, "What is my purpose?" fills our soul in as an empty vessel waiting to be filled. As life goes on, some of us find ourselves estranged from who we used to be. We believe the best days, our glory days, are behind us. With no hope for our futures, we swim in disconnect from the people we truly are. But when asked, "How's it going?" We say, "Fine, how are you?" and walk away. Just to be clear, denying yourself is not your purpose.

Follow me into the Wilderness: A place desolate and dry. A place where you go when life's disappointments have been too many. A place you're not sure how you ended up in. A place that feels dark and lonely and the dreams you once had have been crushed by discouragement. A place where your soul is holding on for dear life wondering if there is any purpose to it living. A place that feels stuck and full of anxious thoughts. What happened? How did we get here? A place so far away from the real you, yet you have no strength to get you back. Where did I go? Why did I go? Will I see me again? A place somewhere along rock bottom.

I now understand the pain that drove me there. I have looked right in its repulsive face. I saw the places of my soul that withered with shame. My soul deepened by the second with weeds of bitterness, twisted and turned into deep, gnarly roots of envy, anger, and fear. Lies upon lies swirled in my brain, a toxic branch clinging to my identity as I surrendered to self-hatred. My heart believed I was an object to be used for pleasure or for someone else to benefit. I saw no identity of my own, no worth or value. The little girl in me walked away and cried in shame each time I didn't stand up for her.

The lies were tucked away in my subconscious "It was your fault," they said. "You did this. You made them do this to you. There's nothing really good about you. You can't speak up because they will hurt us. *No* one can love you. You're so annoying. No one wants to spend time with you. You're a burden. Stop trying; you won't succeed anyway. You're embarrassing. You're not worth *anyone's* attention. Why would they want *you?* You're disgusting; you're dirty; remember what they did to you? Remember all you've done? Yeah, you brought that on. You deserved that. If anyone finds out, they'll hate you. You might as well hate yourself. They won't believe you anyway. Just punish yourself; that's all you deserve: to be punished." These lies began to encrypt the message I would hear for the rest of my life.

As I got older, the little girl in me showed up less and less. She put up her dancing shoes and her joy in a box and instead placed the weight of responsibility on her shoulders that didn't belong to her. She locked up her childhood with a key, and cast it out into the abyss of pain. She had enough, and there she went into my soul, never to be seen again, too ashamed of herself to show up authentically. My survival kit included codependency, addiction, and lust. Desperate for real love and healthy touch, I turned to boys! The attention I received felt like nothing I had ever experienced. It was addictive, and at the same time, I had a terrible feeling that what I was doing wasn't good for me. But I pressed on to fill the void of

attention and nurture. I began a destructive dance, with codependency as my partner, for many years to come. Placating, pretending to be anyone else but me. I was an identity shifter, always catering to whomever I was with to ensure they would like me and not abandon me. I let the people

pleaser come out to play most times; I knew this meant safety. If I just behaved the way others needed/wanted me to, I wouldn't get hurt, and I went
on for years on end, pretending to be "okay." Stuff it in, girl. Don't let it out.
Never reveal. Pain stuffed way down into my bleeding heart; oozing with in-
fection but wrapped in a pretty bow, always anxious that anyone would catch
a whiff of the stench within. I moved swiftly from relationship to relationship,
not ever truly wanting anyone to get too close.

My broken trust of relationships followed me into adulthood as I got
married and had my first daughter. With these new precious relationships
in my life, I was faced with the challenge of remaining the same or seeking
change. Although from the outside I was blessed beyond belief with a beautiful daughter and a great husband I felt I didn't deserve, I didn't consider my
life good enough in my brokeness. In hindsight, I didn't consider me good
enough. I was petrified to allow the gift of their love in my life because if I
really let them in, the pain of their love going away would crush me. What
ran through my mind like a tormenting, a never-ending marathon was my
shattered and broken belief in myself! And my broken dreams and failures.
I had no hope. I didn't want to believe in Jesus or the bible. I didn't grow
up in church so I didn't understand it. My husband grew up in a Christian
home so when we started dating he invited me to church and I never stopped
going. I had attended a Christian church for almost four years pretending to
be a Christian. "Look at me, I'm a Christian. I speak Christianese and no
one would know otherwise. You can finally love me, right?" Remember, recovering people pleaser, identity shifter. (shift-shift-shift). I was a good shifter,
I'm not going to lie! By the way, I could win an Academy Award for all the

performances of my life. Actor to the core, baby! As impressive a Christian character, I had built, I hadn't convinced God or myself into true love and acceptance. I felt even more awkward, alone, and in bondage, to the slew of sin, I had attached my hurting soul to.

2

HEALING THROUGH THE PAIN

In 2014, all the memories of being sexually abused that were suppressed in my subconscious came to the light. I had prayed for healing and it was at this time that I was invited to deal with the monster that held me in bondage and caused me to have so many "issues" that I thought were of my own doing, like cutting myself, addiction and an eating disorder. I was invited to look in the eye of the problem and deal with it rather than try to pretend it wasn't there.

The destruction of ancient ruins. Can you picture a desolate city of ruins with me for just a minute? Let's imagine the Mexican ruins. Imagine with me these massive structures as the places in our soul. And although these Mexican ruins are beautiful, let's imagine them in horrendous shape, for my sake, right now. I know you're creative and have a beautiful imagination!

Yes, picture them with me; see them in utter destruction with horrible words written about you and me on them, the lies of the enemy stamped for us to remember our past failures and mistakes. Graffiti of the lies on the walls becoming the very essence of who we are.

When we suppress and repress abuse, trauma, fear, and emotional pain, it begins to house destruction and former devastation in the ruins of our souls. The subconscious starts believing we are these lies, and our lives reflect what we believe about this world and ourselves! With each unresolved conflict adding to them and making a place for more toxicity in our lives. Generation after generation of sin. Can you imagine that every time you have a toxic thought, it gets added to the walls of your sturdy ruin, fortifying the belief that you indeed aren't worthy? You indeed are insignificant. This was my soul at the time of entering the Wilderness. Poison all up in these ruins, devastating all the good soil of my city. For so long I had suppressed and repressed *me*. My feelings, my desires, my pain. Nearing thirty years of age, I desperately wanted and desired to be different. I knew I wouldn't be able to change something if I didn't understand it. So, with God's help, I plunged deep within, like a Mexican diver off a cliff, just straight down to the root of my problems. I started journaling my feelings, talking to loved ones about my pain. I got prayer from church friends I trusted. I began digging into the word of God and doing bible studies that pertained to what I was feeling. I started praying that God would show me the next step in my healing, and he always did. He would either direct me to a book, a bible study, a Bible verse, a song, a movie in which I could relate to the story and it would help me sort out my own. When I felt afraid, which happened *a lot* during the Wilderness, God's

Word encouraged me that "He goes before all things, and in him, all things hold together" (Colossians 1:17). He held *me* together, the precious child he'd created, but those ruins that held the strongholds of lies of who I was—those he is demolishing to nonexistent rubble.

He took some mighty bulldozers wrapped in his truth, his Word, and knocked those strongholds down! He demolished every pretension (every claim from the devil that I was far too unclean to be loved—his claims that I was unworthy of God's love—he never had any evidence; I just never knew how to fight the enemy back). Now I do because of the example I found in two amazing Christian authors, Beth Moore and Joyce Meyers! They both taught me to speak out the word of God! I take every problem I am facing and I find scripture that correlates with it and I meditate on it constantly and when I can I speak it out-loud! The word of God has saved my life, it's been my healing medicine, it's been my comfort and my delight! I want nothing more in my life than to leave a legacy of a healing woman returned to her father in heaven and redeemed for many to see the glory of God.

While the destruction of the ancient ruins began, I had such a toxic view of myself and the world. As I entered The Wilderness, everything felt so different, desolate, painful, anxious. I walked, not recognizing anything about myself. We began in destruction because none of my core beliefs matched the knowledge of God; all of my thought patterns were toxic, and I needed a clean slate. A demolishing, uprooting, cleansing, and re-laying of the foundation of my core belief system. In hope, I walked forward each day, dreaming of the day the new Libier would arise: planted in healthy soil, based and matching my true identity, when God crushed the bricks of those ruins, and I felt emotional pain like never before that sent me into PTSD (post-traumatic stress disorder). With each crumble of fatal rubble being torn down, my soul ached. He held me together. Never let me go.

I cracked. I opened. I was vulnerable, for everyone to see. At least for the people who were in my life at this time. I no longer cared if anyone liked me. I was seeking my mental health and knew some couldn't handle my mess. I needed to heal. I was healing. It just looked like destruction. For an entire year, I endured PTSD, it was the wildest thing I've ever been through. Feeling like you were just at the place of the deepest pain and suffering you've ever been through and it feels like it's happening all over again. You can see, you can hear, you can feel what caused you to feel unsafe and marred. Something takes over your brain and you are no longer a rational thinking person, you come into a place of panic in which you feel you will never escape. It was in those desperate moments of sheer terror that Jesus became my ever present help. I felt a juxtaposition every time I endured PTSD in The Wilderness. I knew God had me! A part of me knew he wouldn't let go and I was able to endure the pain and suffering to come out from under its control, with a little more freedom each time.

Panic attacks, severe anxiety, and crying pretty much every day, the whole time. Just ask my husband. I'm not even using my Mexican swag-passion right now. I did. I cried. I flipped out. I felt emotions I didn't know a person could feel. I was no longer the Libier of old. However, I wasn't Libier 2.0 yet, either. Who was I?

This mid-state felt so uncomfortable. Wild. As God gave me memories I'd rather not speak of, I saw my self-esteem wither away with each blow

10

of repressed memory brought to my conscious . God was ready for me to deal with those traumatic moments, and it was his all surpassing power within me that allowed me to endure such pain without going off the deep end, for good. I believe, without a shadow of a doubt, that if you pray and trust God an ounce, he will lead you to the places that need healing deep within you, as you can handle it, so that you'll be free to be who you truly are. His! A precious child of God who is loved, cherished, wanted, forgiven, and *free*! Sometimes for me trusting him meant praying and reading my bible instead of doing the toxic coping behaviors I'd come so accustomed to. Sometime trusting him meant being angry at what I went through and yelling at him directly, "Why did you let this happen to me?" I would yell and scream as I processed through these painful emotions! Sometimes trusting in him meant allowing my husband into my pain so that he would know my behavior that day had nothing to do with him and everything to do with a raw heart that was hurting like it had never before. Sometimes trusting God meant not attempting to do something harmful to myself but instead saying, "I am grateful for all that I have been through, I trust that you will have a plan for it." Even if I didn't truly feel grateful or trust. Trusting God started there, at the intersection of gratitude and faith. If God said he was who he said he was, he would take what was meant to kill me and use it for my good. All of those awful memories were already there. I had already been sexually abused, I felt like my innocence had already been taken. I wanted a different approach rather than feeling powerless and victimized. Sometimes trusting him meant weeping for the little girl inside me and allowing all that hurt to just come out of my body. Sometimes trusting him meant getting one foot off my bed to go make sandwiches for my family even though my aching soul was physically affecting my energy and will to live. Sometimes on really bad days, trusting God meant taking one step on my knees and crying on the floor.

I love this quote that pretty much described me in a nutshell at this time. It's by the brilliant Cynthia Occelli. "For a seed to achieve its greatest expression, it must come completely undone. The shell cracks, its insides come out and everything changes. To someone who doesn't understand growth, it would look like complete destruction."

The pain that I was desperately avoiding was the very pain that set me free.

3

THE COURAGE TO CHANGE

My inspiration for change at this season of my life looked like an adorable four-year-old, full of joy and innocence I had never experienced before! My daughter Madelyn helped me see inner parts of myself I didn't know I had. She looked *just* like me! I felt as if I were staring at my four-year-old self. Tripped me out! Then my little Haylee was born and she was as innocent as they get. A brand new baby. I had two lives I had to fight for. I was listening to a Beth Moore YouTube video, and she said that if we don't change, our children will walk just like us, even if they never experience the trials we went through. That thought scared me to life! To think that my girls where going to walk just like me shook me to my core. Like heavens would I allow this to happen. Looking within helped me understand that the wounded *will* wound others. I was wounded and didn't want to continue the cycle.

I wanted to draw a line, *a big line* in the sand and say, "No more; it ends with me." I realized that if I didn't change my toxic and destructive ways, they would spew out onto my precious family. I was so afraid to stand up to the pain, though—terrified that no one would love me after they knew how badly wounded I truly was. Subconsciously, I think I was afraid that I would kill myself because of the shame I felt. Having believed for so long that I was the reason I was abused, rejected and abandoned. I was afraid I'd find out who I really was and hate *myself* even more. So much sin, so much fear. So many past mistakes and failures. So much abuse. How could I walk with my head held high? I was a shell of a girl pretending it was all okay until it wasn't. Until the monster of self-loathing couldn't be contained any longer, and it was taking my life away from me. Until God gave me daughters to love and showed me he loved me like the love I felt for them, except more perfectly and more intensely. This love encouraged me to enter into healing: a love so deep that I was willing to endure the pain of it all. Thank you, Madelyn and Haylee, for the courage you've inspired within me.

My other huge inspiration was my steadfast husband, Doug. If I a being honest with you, it has taken me a long while to trust Doug. Not because of anything he has done. My broken relational mechanism followed me into my marriage. It's only through the trial and testing of our vows through this difficult time that I have seen my husband's character. He loved me in a way so deep, in a way so real, through all of my pain. His love and acceptance of all that I was, even the extreme broken parts, helped me to start to trusting in men. I saw the love of God through his love for me in times when others would have left, he stayed and fought for me and with me. He encouraged

14

me to love those who hurt me even through our pain. He was always so quick to forgive me when I lashed out at him when my heart hurt so bad from the wounds. He was always so quick to forgive me. He inspired me to keep getting back up, no matter how much pain I was feeling.

Lastly and most importantly was the inspiration my heart received from God. His glimmer of hope that my life wasn't over yet. A glimmer of hope that I still had a purpose and a life of dreams in my future. As a little kid and onto my early adulthood, my hope was to become a movie star. I truly believed that when I achieved that goal, I would no longer feel this vast and consuming sense of unworthiness and shame. I felt I never mattered to any-one, so when others saw how talented and successful I had become, I would finally love and be able to accept myself. My self-acceptance started in The Wilderness. God invited me to look deep within and start healing, holding very tightly to my hand. I can now sing for joy that I am coming out into my promised land for good. Into a land where I am free from shame and fear. For me, the Wilderness has meant healing through the pain. It's been wild, to say the least, and very painful, to say the most. However, I wouldn't have it another way. T. W. (you see what I did there?) helped me to love, appreciate, and accept myself as I am. I have seen the face of God—well, not literally *the face of God*, but you know I mean! As a passionate Latina, I am going to be full of emotion, a lot, throughout this book; let us all be okay with it! I call it passion! But seriously, I met God in the midst of the most emotionally painful season of my life. His Word (the Bible) encouraged me to move forward each day in hopes that my life would turn. He was the ultimate inspiration for my healing because he was one I could count on 100% unlike my daughters and my husband who are people and have the ability to disappoint just as I do, God could sustain me on the days when people were unable to.

I hope that my courage will encourage your walk. That you may know you have a purpose so special, God gave his life that you would have yours back! Fuller and more vibrantly than you could've ever imagined!

4

#MEXISWAGPASSIOOOON

I am from Mexico. I was born into the Davalos-Guizar family. My dad's name is Martiniano and my mother's name is Lilia. #MexiSwagPassioooon! I have a beautiful sister named Abigail and two brothers, Ivan and Fabian, who are all pretty much my parents because I was the Baaaaaay-bey! My mother waited nine years to have me after Ivan was born. So very much the last and almost "only child" in the family. My siblings had already grown up while I was still growing, and they loved to boss me around. They used to tell me I was adopted. Here's where my trauma started! Ha-ha! My family is loud and funny and full of #MexiSwagPassiooooon. We are all artistic in some form. My parents met dancing, and most of my good memories from childhood had to do with dancing and laughing, a lot. With my family, you didn't ever need an invitation to come to the party. "Oh you're breathing today? Let's throw a party!" they say! "And everyone's invited! Your cousin, your momma, and daddy can come!" We would have parties and end up not knowing most of the people there. When I first married my Doug, he didn't understand that you didn't need to RSVP to come to the party and if you wanted people to show up at seven o'clock at night, you told them to come at five o'clock or four o'clock, depending on how severe your family was in being late. My warm Mexican family that did the best they could, with what they had. As any family there was a lot of good in us and a lot of dysfunction as well. I believe all families might be different, but we can all relate to somehow being flawed, and we are *all* capable of disappointing one another. Nonetheless, I love my family immensely, and God has given me the desire to honor them and be so grateful for who they are. As is. However, now instead of pretending there was nothing wrong with my upbringing, I'm being courageous to challenge the dysfunction I experienced in hopes to heal and not pass it down to another generation.

Before I wrote this book, I asked both of my parents for their blessing to write our story. It was so important to me to honor them in that way. Many of the wounds I struggled with came from choices they made as I grew up and how I assumed they had to do with me. The enemy twisted my wounds into infectious false beliefs at my core. God is helping me to forgive all the wrongdoing of *everyone* that hurt me. So I write out our story with their blessing.

When you're a little kid, you can't understand that when people hurt you it's a reflection of how *they* feel, not who *you* are. So yes. My family and other people in my life disappointed me.. They behaved in ways that were abusive, unjust, hostile, violent, neglecting, and selfish—and the backlash of those choices wounded my *corazonzito*, but if you look deeply and closely at *their* hurts, it was never about hurting *me*. Although that's the way little Libier saw it. *It's **because** of me*, I thought. God has given me eyes to see my parents and others that have hurt me as human beings who make mistakes! "As it is written: 'There is no one righteous, not even one'" (Romans 3:10). In fact, me being a parent and coming up against my own issues and weaknesses helped me understand my parents a lot more. If God can forgive me for my shortcomings I have toward my children and I can give myself grace for acting unjustly in times of deep pain, why wouldn't I desire to forgive others? I truly believe no one wants to be awful. I truly believe in love, and love never wants to hurt. But I also believe we can all suffer from pain so deep that we aren't ourselves in that moment. I am not excusing wrong choices or saying those who make them shouldn't have consequences for their actions. I believe in consequences. But can you tell me of anyone who has lived a perfect life without ever doing something wrong? The only one is Jesus, and he did it in human form so that you and I would have a friend to know how it feels to suffer greatly. When our hearts are hurting, we don't make the best choices. That's why I'm so passionate about writing to you on how God helped me process all that pain out of my heart. Because even when it's not meant for you, if it affects you, it's painful, and it's imperative to allow yourself your feelings and grief of whatever you've lost. Pretending your pain is not there will only cause more pain in the long run. The only way through is through!

So thank you, Mami and Papi, for your willingness to put your stories out there even though it might be hard to talk about. Thank you for all you *did do* for me!

They've given me their blessing to talk about their pain, and God has given me the desire to honor them and love them through this book.

But we're gonna get real about the pain I felt because it's important.

5

AMERICA

I was lonely a lot. My father was lost in alcoholism, and my mother was more of a single mom trying to raise four children with a husband who wasn't emotionally present. I can't even imagine both of their pain at that time. They both did the best they could, but I remember feeling very, very, lonely as if I was fending for myself. I remember always feeling like a burden of sorts as if I had no real place of safety. Many times when I would try to explain how I felt, I would feel as though the response given to me was sending the message that I deserved everything I was experiencing. One of the moments that marked my heart was when my dad left our home in April to move to America. I woke up and he wasn't there for days. Then weeks. Then months. Then a year. My heart tore more and more each day as I imagine I hoped he'd be around the corner, even if he was drunk and mean, I just wanted to see him. I try to put myself as an adult in my little girl shoes because I often can be so calloused at the events that I felt trauma in. Seeing my daughter's right now at the same age I experienced this, softens my heart toward myself. If my husband were to leave us right now, I can imagine they'd be absolutely heartbroken. As an adult, I understand the complexity of my dad leaving home, but to my six-year-old self, it seemed as if he just left us. *Me.* Because I was a burden. When my dad left, we had to move abruptly to another city in Mexico. I remember my mother being worried because we didn't have any money. Money. It has a way of making you feel one way or another, doesn't it? The interesting part is that money has truly no identity: it's neutral. Yet the lack or abundance of it can shape us rather particularly. It's the thoughts of money that gives it meaning deep within our soul. For me, money represented hurt. Lack. Worry. So money became the thing that I always needed, and somehow when I had it, it always seemed to "slip" right out of my hands. Hello dollar bills, yo. Goo'by dollar bills, yo.

In the interim from when my dad left for America, and when my mother and I immigrated to America, I got a job at a grocery store making tips as a six-year-old bagger. Can you say, hustler, baby? My mother tells me that we needed me to have that job to make ends meet. At that time, I just thought I was working for fun. Being a kid is awesome. Even when life throws you big curveballs, you somehow have an attitude of resilience. It wasn't until I became an adult and realized what I had grown up with wasn't the "norm" that I knew there must have been some issues from the situations I faced that needed to be addressed. But as a kid, I don't recall ever feeling poor or broken; my mother did a great job at keeping the mood light. I can't really remember much of that time. That was my issue. For a really long time, I couldn't remember hardly anything from my past. Anyway, after almost a year of my dad leaving, he sent money for us to come to Sacramento, California. So we moved. Across the world, it seemed!

It was the Fourth of July, 1992, and I was on a Sacramento bound airplane singing, "Pollito, chicken. Gallina, hen. Lapis, pencil. Y pluma, pen." Approximately the only English I knew. But it was all I needed to get started learning this new language that would become a love of mine. When I first got into school, I could not understand one lick English. Oh, it made my head hurt so much to be in a classroom with peers whom I couldn't understand. All I heard was, "blah, blah, blah!" There was an amazing teacher named Mrs. Helfrich who decided to stay after school with me to teach me how to speak the language. I am so grateful for her sacrifice. I don't know what that meant for her, but the time and attention she gave me really shaped who I am today. I love her example because it shows me that we all can do our part in changing the world. It doesn't require months of time, or enormous amounts of money, or even traveling across the world to save the world. We can all do our part to give a bit of our ordinary time, talent, listening ear to someone, **today, right where we are**. Kindness and goodness have a ripple effect. So thank you, Mrs. Helfrich, for your time, energy and love!

Moving across the *universe* didn't seem like a big thing then, but now looking back, I see how much courage it took for my mother to bring me to America. I can't even imagine what she was feeling as our lives had no certainty sitting on a plane having left all we owned and packed two suitcases to reunite with my father. We lived with a cousin for a while their family was kind enough to allow my dad, mom and I to crash their two bedroom apartment. They were a married couple with two little kids, I'm sure it would've been a lot more comfortable for them to live on their own. But with their kindness to share their home, we were on our way to the American Dream. It started a little *"glamorous"* digging through trash cans at the apartment complex we lived at. We found an amazing little mattress we slept on and it was the most comfortable thing in the world! Yes, we found it in a trash can, but as the old idiom says, "One man's trash is another's treasure!" We couldn't believe what amazing things people threw away! We didn't have to dig for long, for one thing is sure. My dad, as broken in alcoholism as he was, always made working and providing for our physical needs for my mother and I a priority in his life. So this began what I truly call the American Dream. A land where you prosper if you work and believe.

I just didn't know that my dreams were going to take some time to come true. That I was going to be refined in the fire first. As life got settled in America, I remember opening up to a friend in elementary school about the abuse I had endured as she and I played at my house. The horror on her face and disapproval (so it seemed) made me shut down completely from ever trying to tell my story. And that's the last time I can recall ever talking about it. There was huge devastation and hurt and so much emotional pain I didn't know what to do with, so I started cutting myself. It felt like relief. When my home life felt unpredictable and unsafe I cut myself to show me that I **was** hurting. Even when I moved to the land of freedom my soul became more bound.

6

MADRE ISSUES

Our situation at home didn't change for many years. My father remained an alcoholic and my mother got fed up. She left my dad. She and I started living on our own when I was in highschool. I thought this was my freedom. But my mother decided *she'd* had enough time sober with *her* pain and resorted to alcohol and pills to distract from all the trauma she'd endured. She struggled with fibromyalgia and chronic pain so she began seeking medical help now that she had medical insurance through her work. It was good in some cases that she finally could see a doctor, but it made things horrible when the psychologist prescribed a bunch of medicine for her to "cope" with her issues, rather than working toward resolving them soberly. All the pain that was in her heart was spilling over to her body, and she kept trying to just fix the body without paying attention to the heart. I was just a kid and had no clue how to help. The medicine was affecting her more than I could understand, and her rage hit me as I handled the pain of her abuse, *soberly*. I already knew what it was like to have the rage of an alcoholic father; I just never imagined I would have to deal with my mother struggling from that as well. I was irritable and frustrated most of the time with her. I wished so badly that there would be something I could do to take away her pain. Nothing seemed to help her. I kept feeling the weight of not being enough as a daughter. I didn't know who to talk to. No church community existed for me at that time. I felt alone and scared. I lived by myself with her, and I know *now* that what she was going through had to be excruciatingly painful, that she needed to be heard and empathized with, but not by me. I was never meant to be her help; I was her daughter. She needed God, a great counselor, and hope. I wasn't and could never fill that. But try, I did. I made it my fault she was in the state she was. Maybe if I loved her *better*. Maybe if I did that *one* thing right. Maybe if I didn't *need* so much space. Maybe if I was not *me*.

I honestly don't know how to explain my faith beliefs at that time, but I didn't think there was a loving God out there, not with how much pain I was in. She just never saw me. It seemed as if she was the only one who's pain mattered. So I was angry. Angry with everyone, especially myself. The "pretend" lighthearted Libier had faded away. Now I was just rebellious and didn't give a crap. About anyone, especially me.

My mother's pain hit a new level. On a beautiful morning on February, 27, my twenty-one-year-old self woke up to my breath being ripped from my lungs. I opened the door to my mother's room and I saw her body laying in an odd manner. I wanted to quickly say goodbye so I could head out the door. After what seemed like an hour of trying to wake her up, I began to feel desperate not knowing what to do, so I yelled, "Mami, Mami, Mami!" I shook her body, and she didn't respond. I heard a knock at the door. A woman from her job was looking for her. Looking back, I think she was an angel; no one ever came over like that. She saw how worried I was that my mother wouldn't wake up, and she asked if she could come in to help me. After seeing my mother, she advised me to call 911. I was supposed to go play Ariel that day in *The Little Mermaid*, for goodness sake! I was on my way out the door to go and be *the little mermaid* at the community theater, and instead, I got in my car to follow an ambulance with my unresponsive mother in it. Everything became blurry, and my brain turned to mush. They took her to the emergency room where I was told by the Doctor, she would never wake up; she lost too much oxygen in her brain because she overdosed on alcohol and pills.

She tried to take her life.

My mother was dead.

So I thought.

I prayed. I *think* my first "real" prayer.

If there's a God, please show up now.

Three days later in the ICU, without it being arranged, a rabbi, a priest, and a pastor came into her room and prayed over her, *at the same time*! No this is not a joke, folks! And the next day, she woke up! Tell me that's not the first miracle I can remember and recognize! I received some cards and people's love at this time that planted seeds of the love of Christ. He comforted me through two people I knew at that time who were amazing Christian people. Sam and Elise, thank you for your kindness and your boldness in faith of God to sustain me with the comfort you yourselves had received from him in your time of need!

I look back at that hopeless week in my life and to be honest with you, the pain of it was what softened my heart towards the idea of believing in God. It's often at our weakest moments that we can allow the idea of a savior in our heart. God is restoring in me love and compassion for my mother. I was so angry at her back then and sometimes still struggle with feeling resentful for the pain of her actions. I couldn't understand why she wanted to leave me. Why I wasn't enough. Even though I thought at that time it was the end of my life, that I could never recover from such a horrific experience, little did I know this was only the beautiful beginning to my relationship with a magnificent God. He held me in the most precious ways, and now when I looked back at this trauma, it was as if I needed it to jolt me into recognition that there was something better for me. It was the gorgeous start of a new life discovering who God was for myself. Discovering who I really was. My mother has been hailing from all the hurt she endured in her life. I have seen the transformative power of love. I have been able to seek to understand her and have compassion and empathy. There is so much hope for what seemed to be tragic.

7

VIVIENDO LA VIDA LOCA

I moved to Los Angeles in 2005. I was convinced I would one day become a movie star. For those of you who don't really know me, I will have you know that ever since I have any recollection of thought, I've *always* felt as if one day I was going to be famous. I love being on stage. I love to dance. I love to act. So clearly, I'm destined for stardom, right?

My whole childhood, I had people around me telling me I had a unique talent. I myself think I'm talented at certain things and I've always had that dream of graduating high school and moving to the big city and making it *big*! But I've also questioned God, why he gave me this *deep* desire to entertain, *why* then, oh, why has there never been any real opportunity for me to become a famous movie star?. I used to have a sense of entitlement.

"My life has *not* been easy, so I *deserve* a big break. I have some talent, so I deserve to be a famous Hollywood star. If I were rich and famous, my problems would go away" I used to think. I would give my family the life they deserve. I would adopt babies from Africa. I would give so much money to the poor, yaddy-yaddy-yadda. What I've come to find out about the precious present is that there is always something to be grateful for in the very moment we are in. If I am giving now, I'll be giving later. If I have an abundant mentality I will also later. If I don't choose to embrace problems in life, I will feel frustrated and defeated. There is always going to be something challenging. But now I get to embrace the feeling rather than resist it. And I've learned that I create my life by the words I speak. And back then when I moved to L.A. I was speaking a lot of defeat. No wonder things never worked out the way I envisioned them. I thought my dreams would just poof into existence. I didn't know I had to work at them, *every day*. I realized what I was really searching for in being famous was the world's approval. If I became well known, it would validate how "talented" and "cool" and "pretty" I wanted to *feel*.

When I moved to Los Angeles, my great friend, Pookie, we'll call her, allowed me room and board at her house where she and her boyfriend, plus a couple of other guys lived. They had room for me under the stairs. Yep. I said *stairs*. I just burst out laughing to myself because I sound like a Mexican Harry Potter with no magic powers. I had my suitcase and the things my Madre sent me to fulfill my dream: a jar of coins, toilet paper, and cereal, which one of the roommates ended up eating as soon as it was in the pantry! Ha, I was so flippin' mad this dude swooped on my cereal. I can't even remember what kind it was . . . it was that traumatic! After the angry first couple of days without my cereal, I settled in my new home. I didn't even care about the small space; I was very grateful for my friend's hospitality! She even got me a job at a local theater in the box office. Ekkkkk! Stardom! I was *almost there!*

I was so gullible to the point that I got myself into some pretty scary situations. I told *everyone* who asked why I was there. I had arrived to become a star. I told this to a man I met at the bank, and he knew I was prey. He asked me if I'd like to come with him to a meeting with an "acting agent." He was sure they'd sign me right away. So I said I would come to the meeting and gave him my number. We texted back and forth, and he said he'd pick me up and take me to the meeting. I felt uncomfortable with the request and told him to send me the address. *I'll be going on my own, thank you very much.* I decided to ask a friend I had just met to come with me. We got to the location, and it was some warehouse, desolate and not at all an "agency" as I had been told. The so-called "agent" was drunk and smelled hideous. They took us on a tour of the shop, and they had beds upstairs. As I am typing this, my spirit is heavy to see what my desire to "make it" brought me to experience. Even though I wasn't very connected with God at that time, he had his guardian angels on both me and my friend. We decided to leave, and the guys let us go. I can't even imagine what kind of situation that actually was. That's the trouble a lot of us girls go through in search for our dreams. Well, it doesn't have to be that way. There is another way! In whatever way God has gifted you and called you. "He has plans to prosper you and not to harm you, plans to give you hope and a future" (Jeremiah 29:11). You do not have to compromise yourself and do something for the sake of a dream. You have the power to say no to anyone who is making you feel uncomfortable. And I believe with

100% certainty, If you submit your dream to God, he will guide you in the right path. Sometimes you will go through difficulty but God will never lead you into sin. If you find yourself there, however, God can *always* bring some good out of a bad situation!

That was the first scary thing that happened to me in the pursuit of my dreams. Then a few weeks later, I was raped. I felt as if the assault had been *my fault.* I asked for it. I said no, but not enough times for him to respect me. *"There you go, you did it again, gave yourself to someone else."* My mind thought.

You did not, baby girl, it wasn't your fault.

After the assault, I went to sleep in my car. I slept with fear for my life, and the minute I could see the sun breaking through, I drove home, devastated. Feeling like the biggest failure, the biggest slut. I remember as I was driving listening to Coldplay: "I will fix you," and tears streamed down my face. Hot, never-ending tears for so much. I thought I would never stop crying. Broken life, broken dreams. I didn't understand why—if I had all this passion for being an actress—it hurt so bad to go after it. I knew something had died within in me. I had *no* hope because, at this point in my journey, I didn't know God. I just felt lost, broken, used, and so scared. I came home to Sacramento and set out to build a "normal" life, a "safe" life, and I didn't know it then, but I set out to *never* follow my dreams again. When I got back all I wanted was safety.

8

#MARRIEDLIFE

When I met Doug, a funny and charismatic- but very serious young man, I wasn't sure if he liked me or not. I didn't know because he didn't try to sleep with me; he didn't ask me for my number. Nothing. He just farted as he was leaving our first double date. At that time, farts were my love language, you could say. He had me at, *"threwwwppp"*. You're welcome. That was my very best attempt at writing out a fart sound. I hope it worked for you, if it didn't, trust me, I can make a much better one with my mouth. I can show ya! Anyway, when I met this young man, he treated me so differently than any other boy I had ever met. It was almost off-putting. But God knew he was the one I had to marry, so he did everything in his power to get me to date him but not try to sleep with him. In my head at that time, I had no conviction of having premarital sex. I had no recollection of the abuse as a kid, but I knew I was off a little. I just felt like I was the problem. And in a lot of ways, I was. I had chlamydia at the time I met Doug. It helped me to slow my roll in that department because I was suffering a very big consequence for sleeping around. I felt so humbled and embarrassed. But at the same time this was probably one of the reasons we were able to make it through the beginning stages of dating without me fleeing the scene because Doug wouldn't sleep with me due to his "religion".

One of the indications I felt as an adult that I had suffered some abuse was the amount of promiscuity I displayed as a young, young teen. My first consenting sexual encounter was at thirteen with a boy who was seventeen. I had *no way* of knowing if this was a good choice. To be honest, I was desperate for love and healthy touch, so I resorted to a cheap substitute that put me at risk for predators time and time again. There was something in me that felt as though I would be valuable if a man loved me. So in my desperation to feeling worthy of love, I gave myself physically, time and time again. With each time, I could feel my soul dying a little more. Feeling my dignity diminish, each time. Being temporarily satisfied (not even) only to go back to cutting myself and being in a state of deep despair. While I looked fine on the outside, my insides were a different story.

So back to Doug, a guy who would love *me*, Libier, not just my body.

I didn't like him at the beginning of our friendship because he wasn't after my tail. Talk about the devastation of abuse and pornography in a mind. I had been so hurt that I was objectifying *myself*. God got ahold of me when I went back to old habits to prove to myself that I was sexy, and since Doug wasn't really "into" me (please realize that Doug was being a *respectful gentleman*), I went back to an old flame because Doug hadn't even asked me for my phone number. We weren't together, we had *just* met, but my ego felt bruised from him not treating me like every other man. One night, my stomach was in excruciating pain, and I had to go to the emergency room. After a few days, I got a phone call from the doctor telling me I had chlamydia, and that was the end of that run with the old flame. I was petrified. I felt so low. I was forced to slow down and not be with *anyone*. God had my attention. I was forced to look inwardly and make a choice of remaining the same or moving forward with God into change.

At this time in my faith journey, I totally believed there was a God. My mother had attempted another suicide in February, two years after her first attempt, and I was sure there was a God in heaven because she miraculously woke up *again*! So yes, I believed there was a God, but I still didn't believe in Jesus or read the Bible, so I wasn't experiencing peace and intimate relationship. I just believed God to be somewhat of a nebulous being. I didn't know him yet, so I couldn't trust him, but at least I recognized he was there! I kept trying to fix myself and my circumstances on my own. But after a lifetime of giving away my dignity, this was the first wake-up call that caught my attention for *good*. To be honest with you, when I got pregnant both times and chose to abort the babies, I had *no clue* what I was doing. Oh, how I have grieved over those horrible choices as a grown woman. Oh, how I have wept over my choices and have repented fiercely. Oh, how I was drowning in feelings of shame and guilt over those careless and horrendous decisions. But at *that* time, since the consequence wasn't threatening to my life, it didn't spur change in me. How horrid is that? Jesus died so I would be free from that. He paid the ultimate price so I would be justified from *that guilt*. What a beautiful savior. I believe un-repented guilt and shame we feel from the bad decisions we make, robs us of the life we came to live. The beauty of the gospel in action rather than in knowledge is *powerful*. Jesus died so you and I aren't swallowed by our sin and the guilt that can so easily engulf us. He paid the ultimate price so that we'd enjoy life in freedom. What a beautiful savior. "Greater love has no one than this: to lay down one's life for one's friends" (John 15:13).

Back to the STD. Well, it certainly caught my attention. I needed a change, and at that time, it meant dating guys who didn't treat me like a piece of meat. So I gave my 100 percent of my attention to Doug even though I wasn't sure if *he* liked me, and he came into my life. God ordained him for this journey with me. My eyes are welling up with tears of joy for what God has given me in my husband. He is not a *perfect* man, neither am I a *perfect* woman. We both struggle with so many issues, but his relentless love for Jesus captivated me. He was so different than the people I had always been around. He was respectful, so kind, quick to say sorry, and he had lightning bolt forgiveness and never made me feel dumb for not believing in Jesus. He led me by *example* in his love for God. Before he asked me to be his girlfriend, he shared three non negotiables with me.

Number one, he said, "I need a woman who is going to put God above anything else." Number two, "I need someone to communicate with me at all times." Number three, "You have to quit smoking." *Gulp*. Was this a business transaction or what? That's my man. He knew what he wasn't willing to deal with and told me straight up! Invited me into his heart and left the hard decision for me to make. No monkey business. I knew where he stood. That's the God-fearing man I received when I stopped trying to do things my way and surrendered *that* part of my life to God, he led me in the way I should go. And we've enjoyed almost ten years of marriage. That's a miracle in my eyes. I never thought I'd be able to trust a man in my life. I never thought I'd be able to willfully submit to my husband. I never thought I'd be able to fight for a relationship so hard as we've fought for each other. God is the reason why Doug and I have remained married, not just as roommates but as intimate friends who love each other deeply, just as we are, while encouraging each other to be better each day out of love. That takes *supernatural* power. It takes the power of the Holy Spirit to love someone through a dark season as Doug did for me.

Doug endured one of the hardest years of our marriage in 2014. I don't think he signed up for this when he proposed to me in 2007, but his love for God carried him through an extremely difficult year with me, and he lived up to his vow to me, for better or for *worse*. Talk about a tested vow. It's so easy to tell someone you'll be with them at his or her worst. Not easy when that person really is in that space. God showed me his mercy and grace through my husband that year when I went from being the "perfect" wife to a mess, in five, four, three, two, one!

9

DEFINING MOMENTS

In August 2012 I was married and had a two-year-old little girl. I felt *safe*. Living life, *safely*. NO running after dreams just relaxing in *safety* and complacency. I had been a "Christian" for five years. I say this with very sarcastic quotes because I accepted Christ into my life for the wrong reason. To be loved by Doug. I was desperate for love and acceptance, and even though I didn't *believe* in Christ or had ever opened up a Bible, I declared myself a Christian. I started acting like the girls I saw at church, and my life on the outside now looked put together. I had found the Lord! I was good! But was I? Let's take a look. I was struggling with bulimia, self-hatred, codependency, anxiety, depression, judgmental as all hell. I wanted everyone around me to act as I heard Christians were supposed to act, but I had no genuine love for myself or anyone else. I was all about that Law Life. A *Pharisee*. I make myself out to look horrible; however, I was doing the best I knew how at that time. I did love God. I just didn't *know* God, so my love fell on a God I had made up in my head based on my jaded spectacles and the things I heard others say that validated the "truth" I chose to believe at the time. Now, I believe that the only truth we can go by is the Word of God, and if you're getting your truth from a source different than the Bible, you aren't getting the richness that comes from listening to God speak love notes to you *through* his Word. His unfailing love changes *everything*. But hey, I was on a journey. I had to go through that to understand the miracles I was about to walk in! We can't really experience God's grace, power, and glory if we think we have it all together. When we can't make sense of the power of God, the mystery of it all creates a healthy fear that is necessary to find wisdom. And I don't mean fear as in boo, be afraid of God; I mean fear as in respect the magnitude and awe of the God of all creation!

Alas, I hit an all-time low. A defining moment in my faith journey and life.

My mother landed in the hospital again for misusing her meds, it was in her hospital bed that she said words that sent me into the deepest depression of my life: "I can't believe I gave everything up for you, for you to have become *nothing*. You're *just a mom*. You've done nothing. You became nothing. You're nothing." It pierced my soul in a way I had never experienced. She was angry because I had just gone to her house and cleaned out all of the pills I saw in her room! I wanted to do something to stop her from continually going down this path of destruction. So she was angry with me and said something hurtful. What came out so easily from her mouth became a belief about myself that took years to heal and shake from my core. At that time I didn't know that people's words were a reflection of the pain they felt inside. I didn't understand that what she was saying wasn't the truth about *me*. I didn't have a sound self-esteem so anytime I was criticized by *anyone*, let alone my **mother**, it weighed deeply in my heart! I felt attached to her emotions and opinions about me. I thought I had to fix her, help her, please her. Little did I know I was on a journey of detaching from her so I could start living *my own life*. I couldn't fix *her*. I couldn't help *her*. I couldn't make myself more lovable for *her*. I finally had to accept I would never be enough for her because she didn't feel enough *herself*. I finally understood I was the one that needed help. I was the one that was in desperate need of tender love and attention. I had made my life about helping her pain that I completely put mine in the back-burner. I never put my needs first. The first part of my healing was recognizing the pain and accepting what I couldn't change and take responsibility for what I could; ME.

So the good Lord has given me such forgiveness toward my mother. I have forgiven her for everything. It has been true freedom. I have accepted that she is a human being and I can't expect her to be a perfect mother. If you don't believe that the devil is downright trying to knock you into a world of fear and insecurity so you won't become who God made you, please consider this: *every* word and action you find insulting to your spirit, *anything* that makes you doubt your worth, *anything* that has made you feel as if it's ripped your dignity from you, *any* painful and hurtful trial that involves sin, is catered by Satan. He will use anyone who is available or *not emotionally available to hurt* you. I *know* now without a shadow of a doubt that my mother doesn't hate me. I know she loves me. She can't not *not* love me. But she is a human being who has good days and bad days. She had a really bad day, and her tongue slipped, and she said something hurtful.

I had been a stay-at-home mother now for two years, a "title" I never thought I would have. At that time I equated worth and value by the title of a person. So you can assume what my soul believed about my work at home, plus the added "encouragement" from my mom, I was spiraling without anyone else being able to tell. I hid my mess so well. "If I look good on the outside no one will know how much my inner turmoil is." Bulimia, depression and addiction were at the right hand of my coping. My Madelyn had already taught me so much about myself without even realizing it. I knew I didn't want to remain the same; I just didn't know how to escape the horror of my new life. I wanted to be okay being at home with my beautiful baby, but I felt as if I was giving up everything to do so, including the very essence of me. At this point, I had not done much in the artistic scene since I had come back from Los Angeles. I had died to the Libier that loved artistic expression! It was over. I felt like a living *dead* person. Merely existing. I still had the same passion, only now the only outlet I had was to prove to *anyone who'd listen* that I was the most perfect, greatest wife and stay-at-home mom in the *history of the world*. I cleaned like a champ. I cooked like a champ. I baked like a champ. I did everything Doug wanted, never letting him know the *real* me. I was frustrated with *him* for oppressing me and having our lives revolve around *him*, yet it was *me* who was unable to speak up about the things that brought me joy. I had forgotten what brought me joy. To be honest with you, I think it was too painful to recognize that I would never get another shot at being a "star." I would watch shows such as *So You Think You Can Dance* and *American Idol* and literally weep from the frustration I felt for not living to my full potential. At that time, I liked to sing, but I was so insecure that every time I opened my mouth to sing in front of others, my throat would close up in fear. The only place I felt freedom was in the ten minutes of worship at church. I knew my little voice would be drowned out in the midst of all the voices singing. So I sang my little heart out. It was like karaoke for God! I was all about that life! I sang and sang, and I could feel God's presence all around me. I felt freedom. But the pastor would start the message, and I would clam up and feel judged for all the sin I had in my life at that time. I didn't understand God's grace. I was so ashamed of the habitual sin I struggled with, and I didn't know how to shake it loose.

I went down a terrible spiral of more self-hatred and bulimia. It was so sad seeing myself wither away in my heart and I always had Madelyn in my mind. "If I don't change, she'll be just like me." At this particular time, my little Haylee wasn't born yet! So I thought about how many "religions" I had given a try. How many books I had read and tested out to see if my anecdote was inside their pages. I realized it was time to open up the Bible and read it for **myself**. To give this Jesus I had heard of so much a chance to show me who he was. I knew the message of the gospel, I just couldn't believe it for *myself*. But on that night, my heart ached so badly that I was willing to listen. My world was crumbling. I considered taking my life; I didn't want to hurt my daughter or Doug the way my mom's actions had hurt me, so I knew that wasn't an option so I opened up the Bible. I told God to lead me into believing him. I turned to Matthew and read about the crucifixion of Christ. I saw it like a movie in my head. If a man who really lived on earth and walked as Jesus did *really* gave up his life for me, with no strings attached, to give me life—if he did it so I could become a new creation in him (2 Corinthians 2:17) and have all the ashes from my life be atoned for (1 John 2:2)—if a man really died so I could have my life back, and all it took was my faith in him to claim my wholeness (Romans 3:22)—if a man like that really loved me with everything I had done, it would change *everything*. I *wanted* to believe. I had nothing to lose and everything to gain if what I heard was true. So right then and there, on my side of the bed, I gave my heart to Jesus. Truly and completely for myself. Not for anyone else's approval. **Just for me**. For my sanity and to see if what he said was true, that he was the God of miracles. So I did it. I jumped in all the way into the awe and wonder of Christ. I wanted to learn as much as I could about the Bible and Jesus and God and the Holy Spirit. And so, my journey began……

10

I SURRENDER

After opening up my heart to Jesus, our family took our annual Summer trip to Forest Home, a Christian family camp in Southern California that we love and adore. At this point in my faith, I felt a little frustrated since I thought something magical was supposed to happen after accepting Jesus and it didn't. I did feel peace now I hadn't before but I still had issues. I thought once I was born again, my life was going to be great! However, in some ways, it was seemingly getting a *little* more challenging. I was still feeling creatively frustrated and I wasn't sure of my God-given purpose. As we settled into our #camplife at Forest Home, I decided to go on a run. I ran because I needed clarity. I ran because it made me feel free. I ran and prayed. I remember with every rustle of my shoes my heart pounding loudly in my chest. I prayed and cried. Have you ever ran so hard you think you might be a cheetah? That was me that day. If only I could see a playback of my actual run to see that I probably looked like a tortoise! Ha! But to me, I was running *fast*. Getting all of my frustration out on the pavement and the earth. I took a turn into the creek at Forest Home. Seeing the vast forest and nature's beauty soothed my soul. I breathed in the clean crisp air and prayed one of the most important prayers of my life. *"Lord, I surrender myself fully to you. I don't know you much yet, but I am grateful that you gave your life for mine. I am ready to give everything up for you. If acting and artistic creativity isn't a part of your will for me please take this desire from my heart. I surrender my dreams to you, if they are not from you, I let them go. I vow to follow **you** wherever you lead"* I am in tears right now at the goodness of God. I felt a sense of freedom after that prayer of surrender. I knew that whatever would come next was going to be really of God. I had faith that he heard my prayer and he would show me what his will for my life was. I surrendered something so precious to me. It felt as if I was giving up **myself** to find **him**. And I was honest and true about it. Deep down inside, I had a feeling God was going to take that dream and that passion from me. I thought for some reason it was a selfish desire driving me wild and mad. So I let it go. I surrendered it all. I finally stopped thinking that I deserved to have a *perfect* life. I accepted that following Jesus might mean heartache and some discomfort. I was willing to go through the pain in order that I might discover more of his love.

Our week at camp ended and we packed up and headed home. I love long drives where I could really talk to Doug. Those moments of amazing intimacy and real conversation have been so precious to me. As we passed many a cow, I told my husband what I had prayed. He said something like,

"Wow, honey, that's a little intense. Let's be in prayer about it. Why don't you consider taking some sort of dance class or something to help you feel artistic." I said I would pray about it, and that was that. About two weeks later, I get a phone call I was *not* expecting *at* all. It was a man named, Sean Farrington, whom I met at church. I had worked with him on a very small film project some years back where I had one or two lines in the scene. He starts the conversation with this info: *He was thinking of filming an independent movie in Sacramento and wanted to offer me the lead role.* Hold up- **Say what?**

I could *not* believe what was happening. I had not auditioned for this, I had not even been looking to be in a movie. At that time, I didn't even have a website, a resume or an acting reel. I felt like I was dreaming and I just listened to him asking him the questions I could muster. I asked him what is it about. He said, "I haven't written it yet." I almost chuckled because I thought, *wow*. This guy was calling me right after I prayed a surrendering prayer about being an *actress*, and he was asking me to be the lead of a movie whose script didn't exist yet. And then he told me there was no budget at *all* for any part of the film. He told me his buddy was lending him a camera, and he had no clue how it would work but felt God's call to make this movie and he really thought *I* should be in it. Doug and I both thought this was too much of a *"coincidence"* to not seek God's guidance about it. We both prayed and after a few days, it felt official that I was to be a part of this independent, no-script, no-budget, movie. My eyes swelled up with tears that God answered my prayer so quickly and miraculously. Not only did he confirm that I was born to be artistic but that in *his* hands, my dreams could become a reality in his time and for *his* glory!

46

I began an adventure that gave me the perfect opportunity to start to *know*ing God and his character. It's hard to see God when situations seem possible in our own strength. We love taking the credit for what belongs to God. Truly all of us are a reflection of his wonderful glory. Some of us recognize it, some of us don't. I was on a faith journey to getting to know my heavenly Father, so he gifted me with a situation that seemed hopeless and farfetched and placed it right in my hands without me being to take the credit for it. It wasn't my talent that gave me that role, it wasn't the city I lived in. Not the school I graduated from. Not a connection. No strings that I could have pulled. It was God and God alone. I needed to see my God in action to begin my belief and trust. It was the perfect space for God to show off! And that he did. I didn't know him at all, but I decided to read my Bible more to discover more! My heart was not ready for what happened next.

11

NINJA IN TRAINING: X'S 2

Sean ended up writing the script for the movie in record time! The role that Sean wrote for me in the independent-movie-that-could, was a bodyguard that saved little girls from being sold into sex trafficking. What? Little me a bodyguard? You know life is funny. I never in a bazillion years dreamt I would *actually* get to play a role like that, but I sure felt I could in the deepest parts of my soul!

I began training in **karate** for the film at a studio near my house. I was learning from two amazing people, Ana and Tony. They both showed incredible talent and discipline! They taught me all I needed to *seem* like I was the ninja the movie I was going to be *starring* in needed me to be! I was on cloud nine! Not only was I able to train in something I had never dabbled in before, like you know, stealing guns from people and kicking folk in the throat. But I was able to have the support of my husband to watch my little darling at home while I filmed. I felt so grateful to my husband for his support and sacrifice! To me, being a part of this project was a tremendous miracle that gave hope to my soul. God heard *me*. Training and being around artistically creative people invigorated something inside of me that had been dead for so long. I felt alive, again!

In the time *between* my prayer and the answer through Sean's phone call, Doug and I went to see *Wicked*, playing in Sacramento. It is one of my favorite shows *of all time*. It was our **third** time seeing the professional production. We are not allowed to see it again for ten years! This time around, however, it was a different experience. I really thought I was done as an artist. I felt like when I surrendered my dream to God he was going to take it away. I was ready for that, but my heart ached so much in grief as I sat in the nosebleed area watching people living out *their* dreams on stage. I wondered if they were truly happy and joyful. I wondered what it felt like. The entire show I cried my eyeballs out! Hot tears pouring down my face. I wanted to believe God was good, I just didn't know what to expect. Fast forward to my kicks at the karate studio, and behold, you had one joyful and grateful little lady! I was overjoyed that God heard me and that he wanted to "give me the desires of my heart because I delighted in him **first**" (Psalm 37:4).

I remember saying to Sean that Doug and I were trying to get pregnant in our initial conversation about the movie. He said, "Okay, that's fine. Just tell me when it happens." **Two weeks after I started training in Karate,** I found myself saying, "Sean, *I'm pregnant.* Do you still want me in the film? Does your ninja have room to be preggo?" Don't worry I told my husband first! Talk about two prayers answered at once. Doug and I had prayed about having a second baby! And here we were about a month into our prayer for expanding our family, pregnant with a little ninja! At that moment I felt very confused. God answered two prayers that kind of contradicted themselves. I was a ninja-in-training as I was carrying a precious child in my womb. How would that play out? Wouldn't I jiggle her too much with my "hay-ias"? For a minute, I thought I was going to have to stop doing the movie. Why would God do that? But after praying and talking with Doug and Sean, we all decided we were okay moving *forward* kicking butt and taking names. We committed to being as safe as we could! I remember Sean praying each time before we rehearsed or filmed that God would keep my baby safe. I knew God's hands were in this because it's in those unlikely moments that you really have to rely on *him* for the strength! I *knew* it was going to be *the* challenge of a lifetime: playing a kick-ass ninja while, in reality, a gassy pregnant woman. I have never feared my gas so much then during a fight scene. Maybe that's how you take down bad guys. Do you just fart in their faces? Thank God I never tooted, out loud at least. My baby made it safely through the entire filming process. I think she actually got her amazingly courageous and audacious attitude from her little baby ninja training she did in my belly! Haley, my darling, I love you and I am so grateful for you. You were the reason this film was finished filming so fast! You kept us on track and accountable for moving forward on the days when we wanted to give up! You're a little heroine yourself, my love.

This movie was a miracle from day one. We had no budget, and *every* time we needed something, we prayed, and God answered. We needed a location. Boom, we got one. We needed an actor. Boom, we got one. We needed a *bus*. Boom, baby; we got one! Sean wrote a bus in the script and one of the actors "happened" to have one. He'd bought it a while back in hopes to turn into an RV and never got around to it, so we were able to use his bus for one of the scenes! *What?* Even to the smallest details, God provided, we shot a scene far from our homes, and Sean needed **one** battery for the microphone, and the actor he was doing the scene with *had* one in his pocket! God can be so funny! He takes delight in showing us who he is when we are ready to listen. He's like, "Look what I can do!" It was amazing seeing God's hand in action. For me, it was God showing me he was trustworthy and I could believe in him even though I couldn't see him. I started trusting a bit more with each God moment!

Now just because this movie was miraculous didn't mean it was all butterflies and unicorns. Some days were so difficult! Filming was hard. Somedays I wanted to quit. I had a baby girl at home, a husband who wanted more of my time, and a growing little bucket in my belly. I was now doing something I had always wanted to do, and yet, some days were really challenging. Being in this season taught me the grass isn't greener on the other side. It taught me that sometimes we fantasize about the future or about goals or successes that we want to attain because we think when we get there—or when we have this or that, or accomplish this and the other—that it will **finally** make us happy, worthy, valuable, or complete. *Nothing* fulfills the way Jesus does. *Everything* is temporary. Even the things people fantasize about: jobs, moving someplace else, a different partner, an important title, power, or money. These things are all vanity, and they are all fleeting. We will never have 100 percent satisfaction and contentment apart from Jesus. We're all left chasing after the wind. Some days are still hard no matter what you do or have realized. I was so happy to learn that lesson. It made me content in the present day. I was living and didn't make me wish I was anywhere else. I believe it's a choice we get to make daily! And yes, some days were really hard, but I didn't quit! We didn't quit!

Being in *Splashed* was so beautiful. It was the first project I had ever worked on in which the leaders prayed before doing the thang. I had never thought God had created us all with purpose, on purpose, and with **specific** talent and ability to glorify his name! It was incredible to see God giving us all strength to do each part that needed to be done to have the film complete. Another thing I learned was that I am not more special than *anyone* else. In comparison to the person who cleaned the bathrooms of the shoot location, we have the same value, and we are *all* needed for the completion of the project. Like a puzzle! I always had this sense of pride about my talents. I was puffed up by ego because I was terribly insecure about my gifts. I *never* considered myself truly beautiful or gifted. I always questioned it in the back of my mind. So I puffed up with my pride and ego to protect myself. And with that came a lot of pride with some of the things I could do. I thought I was better than others based on titles. This film helped me with that. It helped me understand we are all of *equal* value and *worth*, no matter what our "job" is; we just have different skills. It felt so good to feel confident that I could do all things through Christ, and that I wasn't in competition with anyone else. It felt so good to finally feel at peace with myself and the gift of acting God put in me. I was able to have fun and focus on the work rather than questioning if I was **good enough** for the film or my part. I was able to give myself grace in the moments where I made mistakes. This was very unlike me or unlike any other project I had done before. I remember to this day the prayer Sean would pray over us before filming. He'd say, "Lord, God, the gifts you've given us are irrevocable." It helped my soul and self-esteem to hear those words being prayed over me. It made me feel secure to know God knew exactly what he was doing when he put the love of acting in my heart. That I could just be who I was and let others be who they are. That the passion and desires I had questioned all my life were actually from God himself.

I started to read my Bible more and realized God's whole purpose in this season of my life was to show me how much he **loved me**. He freely gave me big and small signs to point to his love. One of which was something that transformed my relationship with my God for all of time. I started learning that to hear from God, I needed to be in his word! I heard someone say, "We have to believe what *God says* about us, **more** than what the *world says* about us." I had this wound in my heart from the words my mother spoke over me: "You're nothing." I acted out on those words, and I didn't want to feel that way anymore. At times, I truly believed there was a God, but my relationship was a little nebulous I believed him as a big God but I didn't understand the rich intimacy of his love until I did a Beth Moore devotional, and she suggested to take any unkind words we've heard about ourselves to God and ask him to replace them with what *He* has to say. I had nothing to lose. I knelt down and prayed that God would replace the words my mother had said about me. I prayed that he would tell me what *he* thought about me. I finished my prayer and got on Pinterest of all things. The first pin that popped up was a verse that said, "I will call the unloved and make them beloved, in the place where they yelled out, *You're nobody*" (Romans 9:25). I have *never* felt the way I felt in that moment. God so quickly answered my prayer and *so* specifically and intimately; I just looked up the pin on Pinterest right now and got the goose willies just thinking about that night that would *forever* change my life. Listen, that night I went from believing in *a* God, to believing God at his precious Word! He was no longer some mean old God who just punish me for my sin, but a loving father so gentle and pure bending his ears toward my cry for redemption and healing. Ready to trade with me treasures for my ashes.

Throughout the filming of Splashed God helped me to believe in his love for me. I had tried to obey him for the sake of obedience for so long, and I had missed out on the amazing adventure he had for me, *beginning* with his love. It starts there and ends there. Because *when* you feel loved, you want to obey, not the other way around. Lasting change for me came when I understood the lover of my heart, his character, and his purpose for my life. I think what God was really training me to be is a spiritual ninja! There is a fight! An invisible fight we all must face on this earth and it's number one attack on your life has to do with one of the biggest questions for a heart, Am I loved? Does anyone care about me. Let me tell you, God cares about you. You are beloved in every way! Be a spiritual ninja, darling! Train like you've never trained so that you can stand tall and discover who you are because when you do, you'll be undefeated. God has the victory for you!

12

DIFFICULT TO TALK ABOUT

"Silly boys, they don't know where their porn is coming from." This was a line that cut through my sin. It was spoken by the antagonist of Splashed. I guess she could have said, "Silly girls." I was at the crossroads of my desire to help end human trafficking and struggling with an addiction to pornography. I had no clue what human trafficking was before starting to film and what a huge problem it was in our world. Not even the world, as in some far away country, but how prevalent it was here in Sacramento. I started learning about my character and the premise of the movie, and the more I educated myself on human trafficking or sex trafficking, the more I became convicted about my addiction to porn. Yes, you can take a minute to reread that sentence. I realized there were girls and boys out there who were in pornography who didn't want to be! I am actually positive that the majority of people don't know how they end up in the industry. Or even at a strip club. I used to judge people who made the choice to give their bodies for money or dance around a pole. God has shown me no one does that without having a gaping hole of hurt in their hearts—those who are in desperate need of the love of Jesus! He showed me my addiction to pornography was due to a huge hurt from my heart, from being exposed to it as a kid when I didn't have a say. But I was all grown up. I could make difficult choices now. And continuing to watch pornography meant I was also aiding in the abuse of the people in them. I was a part of the human trafficking problem. I didn't want to be. So I tried to stop. And I couldn't. I never felt more defeated than when confronted with a habit I had ever since I can remember in my four-year-old brain. So many years of watching images that were never meant for my eyes. I felt like such a strong woman in some ways, yet I couldn't stop something that I now didn't want any part of. What's wrong with me? I thought. I felt so much shame. And I felt so alone. I was this mother wife. I had accepted Christ in my life and now I was beginning a journey to following my dreams again yet I was bound by something that I never invited myself. It was never a problem in my eyes until I tried to heal and make a change. I wanted to take responsibility and no longer remain a victim of my past.

I forgive the people who exposed me, I forgive the people who took the photos in the first place, I forgive myself for struggling with the addiction. I forgive but only through the loving sacrifice, Jesus paid on the cross. I receive the power to forgive and let go of the pain I've held on with resentment and bitterness. I forgive, so I can be free. "I have been crucified with Christ and I no longer live, but Christ lives in me. The life I now live in the body, I live by faith in the Son of God, who loved me and gave himself for me." (Galatians 2:20) My heart is full of gratitude that God knew I had been hurt and helped me to realize that there was so much pain behind my sin. That he saw the pain I had suppressed and he was willing to heal me through his love. and wanted to love me, change me, and then use me for his kingdom. He delights in using broken people so we can see him clearly. I first had to know with all my might how much he loved me, in spite of how he found me (extremely broken) in order to keep moving forward in healing. He kept showing me his love in different ways that were so unique to me; it was very hard to pass as coincidence. He encouraged me to change because he accepted me just as I was, I didn't have to clean up my mess before I came to him, he came to me at my mess and stood with me! He showed me mercy and unfailing love that went deep into the makeup and fabric of my being and he gently shone his light into all the yucky places where I had not let him in before. I knew it would be difficult to change something that had been a norm for me from an itty-bitty age. This was a huge secret in my life and an enormous source of shame. I was so afraid to talk about it with loved ones for I knew that change would require confession to those I loved most so I could be accountable for the change. I felt scared, however, I desperately wanted to believe that, with God, all things were possible. That my dignity depended on him and not on the awful things I had endured as a child. That I could be made new, and all the shame and guilt I felt could be appeased by his forgiveness and transformative love.

Quitting pornography was one of the hardest things I've had ever done in my life! My brain was accustomed to this thing for so many years. It took a lot of faith, dedication to changing my thoughts, and averting my eyes whenever I saw something inappropriate. It required all my surrender and prayer. But I wasn't alone. I had God by my side and people I trusted to share my pain who didn't judge me. They just listened and partnered with me in prayer. If I can be delivered from this, so can anyone. Our world is struggling with such moral deprivation, and I believe a change is coming for dignity and great morals! For purity and a healthy view of sex! I believe that to create the change we must first be that change in our personal lives. I believe to change the tapestry of our overly-sexualized generation we must change the way we view people and ourselves. But I believe before we can make anyone change the symptom of a sex addiction, we first have to address the root of the problem. Lack of love will drive anyone to get what they need from a cheap substitute. Christ is the only one who can fill the void of not having received the nurture and love we all so desperately crave. It is so sad that we want to end sex trafficking, and we'll throw money at the problem, but we don't want to do what will make a lasting change: changing ourselves in whatever manner points to the objectification of ourselves or someone else. It is easier to give our money to a cause and feel better. But money will not deliver us lasting change. People being sick with an addiction to porn and buying sex is what is causing the problem. People seeing others as a means to their end is the problem. Objectifying others and sometimes ourselves is the problem. Not believing how much Jesus loves us and wants to change us, and accepting the challenge of facing a deep pain within, is the problem. Friends, there is healing through the pain. Pain will not consume you, but it will heal you if you go through it with God. It wasn't my fault someone exposed me to porn at a young age and then the devil used this very thing to skew the way I thought about my own sexuality and my worth. But it became my responsibility as an adult to change. Even though it was difficult, quitting porn has been one of the best decisions of my life. I have regained what I lost and so much more!

Some thoughts that kept me trapped in an unwillingness to change were the follows:

No one can see what I am doing! No one would have ever known this about me, so it doesn't matter. It's my choice for my life. Everyone does it. It's not that bad. If I wanted to stop I would.

But God knew, and I knew. You know that the most precious part of it all is? I thought I was gaining something from it. God showed me what riches he'd have in store for me if I gave it up. I looked forward to receiving what God would give me. I didn't even know know the beauty of what he'd given me in exchange for that filth. I've been delivered from it and have been sober from those explicit images for almost five years; my mind has changed about sex. There is a huge difference in how I view myself and other people. I feel an innocence and intimacy with God: the truest gift I've ever received. It was as if I was given back my purity and wholeness. My dignity was something I had never experienced before. That was the best gift I received from letting go of that addiction to something I thought would give me love in return. I still choose to take it one day at a time. Every day I make a choice to keep my eyes averted from impurity. What angers me the most now as a mother of two precious girls is that sex and porn are everywhere. You can be walking with your five and three-year-old in the mall and be bombarded by seductive girls on huge posters right outside a Victoria's Secret. How did we get here? Commercials for a chocolate ice cream bar are explicitly sexual and make my stomach hurt to think my little girls have to grow up in that. Women dancing so seductively during a day show on television. It makes me sick that little innocent boys are scrolling through social media and can come across a naked picture of a woman they did not call out to see. It's everywhere, bombarding our eyes and minds, and if we don't make a change, depravity of this kind is going to kill more than our morals. It starts with a change in one person. It starts with you and me.

If you're a woman on this earth, you've felt the pressure to be sexy. If you're not sexy, you won't succeed. You aren't wanted. Where is our worth? I'll tell you it's not in being sexy. Our worth is in knowing who we are in Christ. I'd even challenge big stars out there who are dancing and dressing provocatively to pursue dignity and be a good example for all the little girls out there trying to follow in their footsteps. I see an oversexualized nation and world that is in great need of Jesus and healing from the inside out. I am obviously not judging here since I was there myself; I just feel passionate about this subject because I understand the pain that drives us to be overly sexual. I honor everyone, and with respect and love, suggest we draw a big line in the sand for generations to come to experience healthy sex, love, and self-worth.

Since I've allowed God to show me the deep wounds that propelled all my habitual sin, and he has come in and cleansed me, I have experienced a peace I have never known. I have a love and respect for myself and my sexuality and body that I never knew before. And I feel a purity in my mind and soul I have never known before. Porn was a cheap substitute for what I was truly craving. I was craving the love of Jesus, acceptance, peace, and wholeness. I couldn't have those things apart from Christ. God has taken this awful thing and turned it into good in my life. I am no longer ashamed of who I was because who I was wasn't the real me. I never knew my identity in Christ until now, and I am who he says I am: redeemed, precious, and lovely in his eyes. He made me have a relationship with him, and in that, I found I belonged without trying. I have love without performance and worth without doing anything to gain or lose it. I have value because he gives it to me as a gift. I am worthy of true love and connection, and I was rejecting God and his love by continuing to avoid my issues face to face. I tried giving up porn on my own, and I couldn't. It was a supernatural blessing that came with my cooperation with God. It took everything in me to cooperate. It took enduring a lot of emotional pain from remembering past abuse. It took so much rewiring of the thoughts that rampantly ran through my head. But God and I did it. And I am all the better for it. I am living proof of the miraculous power of Christ. His love called me, his forgiveness healed me, and his mercy gives me peace.

I never in all my life thought I would really come to know peace. My life had been beautifully traumatic. I'd been shaped by the waves and crashes of life. Fair? Nope. But life is full of good and bad. I am who I am today because of all that I've been through and I love how God has shaped me. He takes broken lives and makes masterpieces! No one is far too gone, no one is an orphan, no one is hopeless, no one is alone in this life! If he can change this little gal typing fiercely on this keyboard, there is hope! His peace transcends even the worst of circumstances!

God doesn't let us experience anything he isn't 100 percent sure we can endure in his strength. "He can work all things together for our good. (Romans 8:28)" Even if we're too prideful to ask for his help, he is always there waiting, probably stepping in like a defense linebacker protecting us from the unimaginable. Things that never came our way because God was protecting us from these horrible boulders coming at us to take us out. Yet we only see what does happen to come our way, and our attitude becomes one of the complaints and "why me" (I'm speaking of my experience. It usually takes me a while to have a thankful attitude toward challenging times). Our minds think our lives are going pretty well because of our own doing. We say, "I succeeded, and that makes me a super, amazing human being." Often, we forget we are amazed to reflect his glory! We are unsure of our worth so pride puffs us up! We pretend to have it all together. Until a real catastrophe comes in and tears us apart, and we are left looking upward wondering where God has been all along. God's wrath is not some fiery hell hole that we have to endure in this life. It is our own choice: not trusting him and not letting him into our daily life becomes his wrath, because apart from God we can do nothing that truly matters. God's wrath is the absence of himself in our life.

It's something we can prevent by just saying, "I'm trying to trust you, Lord. I want to love you with all my heart. I don't know how, but I want you to show me." The tricky part is that we need to be ready for all God must undo, to give us the ability to trust and let him. We have to die to ourselves and make many changes in our lives to truly say we are all in with God. This is not easy. We have to die to ourselves and to all of our preconceived desires of this life. The more we exercise trusting God and having a thankful attitude for the challenges that come our way, the easier it becomes to trust and to be thankful for some "catastrophe." God can bring a blessing in the darkest times. We just need to hold his hand.

A part of trusting God and wanting him to change our hearts has to do with surrendering who we think we are, and who we ought to be. Everything we think we deserve and want is not often what we need. God doesn't mess around. If we're truly coming to him wanting his help and surrendering to him, we have to make a choice to die to ourselves and see what he has for us. Whatever his plan is a thousand times better than what you or I have in mind. Maybe we can't see it yet, but it's there. God promises us good news. He is a kind and gracious God who is faithful and never fails. God has shown me a peace beyond anything I could have ever imagined! Even through my addiction to pornography. Through my addiction to anything that buffers difficult feelings. Through the many times I failed and will fail again, God's peace is something I would not trade for the world now that I've experienced it first hand! You can not explain it. But when you partner with God through prayer, surrender, and repentance to overcome something that seems too difficult for you alone, his unfailing love, forgiveness, and peace flow directly on you and your issues from Heavenly places! Life can break us but God will put us back together much better than we ever were. I want to trust God with all of my heart. I know I don't do that at all times. I admit I need help; I need encouragement. There isn't anyone breathing that doesn't need encouragement, love and God's forgiveness! Even through our wondering. Even through our doubt, and especially through our sin, God will remain faithful! He can not lie. If we seek him and in prayer ask for his help, he will never let us go! No matter what sin is weighing us down with shame and guilt! He paid the ultimate price of sending his one and only son, Jesus Christ, to die for what you and I feel shame over. Will we trust him with the dark places within our souls?

13

PAIN AND PRIDE

I finished filming the movie by God's grace. At that time, I was exhausted: a mom to a fast-moving toddler, working on remodeling a home to move into before we had Haylee. So in the midst of chasing an adorable little girl, painting walls sterling gray, and kicking bad guys while I took away their guns, I developed a hernia. It was one of the most painful things I had *ever* experienced. Mainly because it was chronic pain coupled with an emotional issue of pride. I hated asking people for help. It made my stomach hurt. Literally. I would get an ache in my belly if I ever had to reach out to *anyone* in need of *anything*. I wanted to be okay all the time and not seem needy or annoying. Holy cow. God used this time to show me I was struggling with pride and didn't know how to *receive* help. He also showed me the power of vulnerability and allowing people into my mess and my heart. I found out people can have a *huge* positive impact in our lives. We want to do it alone, but secretly, we wish for connection. We can't have it both ways. And as I heard a great friend of mine say, "The problems we faced in relationship that wounded us will resolve themselves *through* relationship."

The kind things (big and small) my friends did around this time touched my heart in a huge way—from making us meals when I had my surgery to giving me frozen breast milk they had pumped for their own babies because I couldn't nurse my *own baby* for several days after surgery! Those were just a couple of examples that blessed me and showed me that people want to help. They were happy to help. I wasn't a burden. I look back and feel sad at how resistant to help I was. Having a toddler, being pregnant, and experiencing so much pain softened my pride, and through that painful experience, I was able to start receiving from people who loved me. What a difference that made in my life. Fast forward to now. I love receiving of all sorts of things: help, presents, apologies, money for my art, compliments, love. But above all, I can *finally* receive the biggest gift of all: Christ. Think about it. If you have a hard time receiving help from a friend, how much more difficult will it be for you to receive the gift that Christ gave when he died on a cross for you to live a life free of guilt and shame when there is not a single way you can pay him back? I mean, zero ways to measure up. No amount of good works to check off the list to be worthy of what he did for you and me. We could never deserve what he did to save our souls. Yet we have it available to us, by *faith*, and we can accept it at any point in our lives, no matter what we've done. That gift is so precious; I wonder if we are ever truly enjoying its rich fullness here on earth. He wiped away all our sins and says he will remember them no more (Hebrews 8:12), but are we receiving that truly? So after hernia surgery, I accepted my need for help. I can't do this thing called life well **without** the help of my family and friends. And after seeing what happened when I collaborated with amazing people—being able to see their strengths and passions—I *wouldn't* want to do this life alone.

14

AWKWARD PRAYERS

Okay, let's talk about bacon shall we? Wow. We went there! Super deep couple of chapters, right? If you're still with me, very much an optimal high-five to you my friend!

As God was delivering me from so much, he was intermittently working overtime to keep me hopeful. The movie wrapped and I went back to "normal" stay-at-home-mom life for a while, but one fine day I get an email from Sean sending me the trailer of the movie! My heart was beating so fast. I could feel my stomach in my mouth or maybe in my feet. I don't know, *something* was happening to me. So much anticipation and excitement. It had been a while since we wrapped filming so I was excited to see the fruit of our labor! I honestly thought the movie was either never going to actually come out (at that time I was still plagued by thinking negatively, a lot, so I think this was my defense mechanism for not being disappointed!). Or that it would be so horrible I would never want to watch it or show anyone ever in my life! Ha, sorry Sean nothing personal! But when I watched the trailer, I about fell off the chair! It was the first time in my acting career that I didn't bash on myself. It was the first time I felt so happy with my performance. Is it a coinkydink that I had prayer before every take? I think not! Honestly, if you had seen us filming, you probably would have never thought it would have turned out the way it did either. I sat in amazement at the talent of so many folks poured into that trailer. I *saw* how much faith and prayer had gone into it. I sat in bewilderment and my lip began it's quivery thing that happens when *that* cry is about to ensue, you know, the ugly cry where you almost want to go look at yourself in the mirror to confirm that you're in fact crying *that* ugly, cry? Yep, that one. I was blown away and hopeful that the entire film would be as good as the trailer was. What I was more grateful for was the gift of faith God gave me. See, the Bible says that "Jesus is the author and perfecter of our faith" (Hebrews 12:2). For the longest time, I beat myself up because it was so hard for me to have faith and trust God. I had to believe that even in my unbelief, God was still sovereign, and he could work with my little mustard seed of faith and make it grow with each passing day. And that it did. I went from being a skeptic to fully loving Christ because I started to know him through reading the Bible. I was starting to discover that my passions were in line with my purpose, and that made me so joyful! I had dreamed of a moment like that my entire life. To be the "star" in a movie. It wasn't how I had envisioned it: a Hollywood film, million-dollar paycheck, and my face on *People Magazine*.

But somehow it was *better*. God protected it, and I grew in *faith* and character. To me, that was better than gold—not that gold is bad—I believe it's wonderful to get paid for what you love to do. However, at that time, my heart needed a lot of hope and faith in this God I hardly knew and it happened through a little indie movie, without a budget. .The process of the film fulfilled many longings deep within my soul. Being an artist is painful when you're not making art. I was finally making art after a long while of being held captive by fear. Freedom is treasure and I felt rich!

We decided to have a party to celebrate the trailer being done! We gathered at the Karate Studio where we rehearsed all the fight scenes. It was so much fun seeing all the cast and crew and some of their loved ones! We all stood in amazement of the trailer being such great quality. We high fived and celebrated! Between all the nerves and excitement of the night my little one in my belly decided she'd had enough in my womb and the next day my water broke! Almost four weeks early Haylee decided she was ready to be born! After a season of full throttle, God gave me a the precious gift of slowing down and have a newborn. What a precious little gift was Haylee for our family. She was teeny-tiny and felt so delicate. Her life made ours even more lively. My prayers were answered as I was struggling with this extremely painful hernia that she'd come early! God heard my awkward prayers. To be honest with you I didn't know if God would answer a prayer like bring my child out early because I am in so much pain. But he did and she was healthy for the most part! A few scared here and there as the cord was wrapped around her little neck when I gave birth to her and then she had a little bit of jaundice. But, pretty healthy otherwise! We began our new rhythm with two children. It was challenging for the first six months. I can remember crying because I felt so tired. However, this time around, I knew she'd grow up as fast as her sister and this infant stage wouldn't last forever. So I enjoyed my little nugget as much as I possibly could. As I fed her, burped her and changed her poops, the movie made its way out of the editing phase and onto the friends and family screening.

On November 17, 2013, we all gathered in a little church downtown and watched the finished product. Whoa! It was one crazy experience to see everyone's hard work. I was in awe of God and all he managed to do in the time that we had started all of this. All the while, we had *zero* budget, hardly *any* connections to anyone, and the lead karate heroine was pregnant. When there is faith, unlikely outcomes to dire circumstances are possible because God is amazing and can do anything he wants. Trust him for an inch, and he'll give you a gigaparsec. Yeah, I know, I'm making you Google, "gigaparsec" aren't I? I Googled "What is the longest measurement of distance?" Gigaparsec! I love that word! Okay, I'm done! The movie was the beginning of one of the most amazing seasons of faith in my life. A bunch of crazy, unusual things started happening, such as getting to be excited about making it into Action On Film International Film Festival in Southern California. We also got into Sacramento Film Festival, although it ended up being pulled out because we premiered the movie before the festival. Oops! I began to have a part in the post-production with our Splashed team and learned how to produce a movie premier.

At that time, I was doing a Bible study from Beth Moore called *Believing God*. It changed my life to do that study. I love Beth Moore. Girl, if you ever read this, I thank you for your courage and vulnerability. I pray for you, and I consider you one of my spiritual mommas! I love you, and thank you for everything you did in your life. Thank you for your courage to not remain the same! God did amazing things through you in my heart! I love you, Mrs. Moore, thank you! As I delved into the Bible study, Beth asked a great question at the very beginning. "Can you think of any need you might have that would require more strength than God exercised to raise the dead?" If the God who resurrected Christ from death into life is with you—if what you're asking for is in his will for your life—what can he not do? I sat in that chair wondering if God would help us with the premiere of *Splashed*. I had never known how to put my faith in #action! There's a big difference in thinking you have faith and actually putting it into action in your life, right this second! It felt painful to put something so precious in my heart (the desire to have an excellent premier) into faithful action. I felt scared to death for God to not see this through in my way or to be left looking like a fool. To get disappointed. That is why faith is so much harder done than said, because it can be painful. However, it is also one of the most amazing things you'll ever do; once you realize you have a loving father who wants to bless you and not harm you, you can trust in him *more*. You have a father who, even when you become disappointed, comforts you and tells you there is something *better* he's working on. It's never that he doesn't answer a prayer because you don't deserve what you are praying for; it's that he sees your heart and what it is you need at this current moment, but knowing him makes you realize his heart is always loving toward every request you pray through faith. He can edit your prayers and give you his highest and best, *always*! I love this quote from Max Lucado:

"Our prayers may be awkward. Our attempts may be feeble. But since the power of prayer is in the One who hears it and not in the one who says it, our prayers do make a difference." This was truly the start of me putting the very, very little faith I had in this God I was starting to get to know into faith-filled action in my everyday life. At that moment, the premier seemed like a good place to start.

We didn't have a big following at all. No one (outside of our loved ones) really cared we had poured our hearts and soul into this film, and we couldn't think of many people who might have wanted to come see it! We knew the circumstances around it: it was an indie film, with zero budget, that was filmed quickly. We knew we still had a lot to learn about making movies. However, we were grateful we did what we felt called to do, even through the fear of failing. At that time, I didn't even have any social media. No "followers". Just me following my precious Jesus. We thought maybe, just maybe, a hundred people would want to come see it the movie. We booked a theatre that sat three hundred, but when Sean (writer and director) and Laureen (producer) went to check it out, the speakers blew out. You can't have an action film premier with a weak sound system! Our problem became our provision!

I proposed to Laureen and Sean that we take the first step of faith. My thought was that we had God's provision the entire time we were filming. This film and what we were doing with it was in his perfect will. He provided for everything, so I wanted to believe he would also provide a great big ole place for us to premiere the movie we'd worked so hard on! So we took a leap of faith and went after the Crest Theatre, which was way bigger than the other theater and could fit 975 people! *Gulp*. it was also *way* out of our budget. It would take a *miracle* to fill those seats! All we had was about $110, which was way shy of the deposit needed for the Crest. With all our might, we believed the God of the impossible would take care of the details. We walked in faith and made up our minds that God was going to provide the deposit the Crest needed, and as we were going to talk to the owner about it, a friend of mine ended up lending us the exact amount we needed. What a *blessing*! Thank you, Coco; you know who you are. God works in miraculous ways. We booked our spot and prayed and hoped for God to do only what he could do. We knew if we at least got three hundred people to come see our Indie Film, we could break even and pay my friend back, so we prayed for God to do that and more. Secretly, I prayed that it would be sold out! That God would take the message of this film and deliver people from the addiction to pornography and that anyone who had been hurt in human trafficking would come to know his redeeming love! So what happened? We waited in faith to find out.

15

WHAT CHA GONNA WEAR?

About a month before the premier, I was getting all my to-dos checked off, and having a dress to wear was one of them! Ekkk! This was the first time in a long time I had so much excitement in my life that directly correlated to me as an artistic individual. Being a wife was awesome; being a mommy was amazing. But something happens when you forget about yourself as an individual and give all of yourself to those labels. I thought only focusing on my husband, home and kids was a good thing, but I didn't know I was committing creative and emotional suicide. I was a carcass of myself. I looked like myself, but I didn't have any dreams or hope for my future. I didn't even feel as though I mattered. So I gave my everything to my husband and kiddos with no love or respect to myself. .

Please don't misunderstand my heart. I *love* my family. There is nothing wrong with being a good wife and mother and **serving** your family. And in the right moments, putting them as a priority, as God when we serve in love. However, I was trying so hard to serve them out of my scarcity rather than my abundance. I was quickly running out of steam because I wasn't showing up for myself, first. There is something terribly wrong when you are not living the life God gave you and "giving" everything to your family when all you truly feel inside is resentment that you "gave up" your life for them. I learned God made me purposefully with the dreams and hopes inside of me for a reason, and I didn't have to give up myself to be a great wife and mother. God showed me my dreams mattered. My talent and ability mattered. My desires mattered. I mattered. My *needs* mattered. Being selfless isn't about thinking less of yourself. It's about you deciding you are important and giving yourself the time to take care of *you first*, then you can take better care of others after because you're thinking of yourself less. God made you, and he wants you to regard yourself as his workmanship and to treat yourself with love and kindness. Then you can give that same love and kindness away. When you understand who you are, and whose you are, it changes you from the inside out. It makes you valuable in your own eyes, and because you feel valued, you can serve and give that love out! Because you see your value, you don't need your family to convince you or other people or things to tell you that you matter and have worth. If you can't give that to yourself, nothing will. I started taking the time for self-care. I said "no" more often. I spoke up when I needed time to myself. I had my own back for the first time in my life.

Most of us have heard the saying, "You need to truly love yourself in order to give love." What does that really mean in our society when one of the biggest issues now is *self-centeredness*? It would appear that everyone is in love with themselves, right? Second Timothy 3:2 says that "people will be lovers of themselves, lovers of money, boastful, proud, abusive, disobedient to their parents, ungrateful, unholy."

This was a little confusing for me. I come from a past of abuse, and to be quite honest with you, I've struggled with self-hate, low self-esteem, self-harm, an eating disorder, anxiety and depression—oh and also addictions of all kinds—to anything that takes the pain away. Wow. That seemed so difficult to type. My heart goes out to anyone struggling with even *one* of those issues. Listen, God is a master at taking broken things and making beauty out of our ashes. Go read Isaiah 61:3. This verse saved my life as I was falling apart. It gave me hope that God could do something with all the shattered pieces of my heart and somehow turn them into something beautiful! I know now as much as it hurts to admit all these things on paper that my heavenly Father has faith in me. That I will not remain the same. And neither will you, my love. Neither will you. If you have one little ounce of belief of God in your heart, he can and *will* help you. Do not lose your hope when everything seems to be falling apart. If you are in prayer and making sure you do all in your control to surrender to Christ, you will see and experience him putting you back together more beautifully than before.

So with all of that said, back to the dress for the premier! At this time in my life, I had been in a wild rut of wearing yoga pants for years! And most of the time there was no yoga class! I did the getting ready on Sunday to go to church, but I didn't have the desire to give much attention to my appearance in that season for any of the other days of the week!

I thought, *Why bother, I'm at home all day.* So here I was, needing to be red-carpet ready for the premier, and I didn't have anything to wear to the ball. So I prayed for a dress. I had the idea that someone would lend me a dress to wear, so I went to the mall and told my story to several stores. They denied my request. Defeated, I drove home and called a family friend. She directed me to a secondhand boutique named Sequels in Loheman's Plaza. So there I went, to ask again. When I walked in the store, I felt such good vibes. I saw an extremely beautiful lady steaming clothing. I approached her with courage, introduced myself, and began telling her my story. I asked if she owned the place, and she said yes, so I asked if she'd let me borrow a dress. I can still remember her now. Her sweet demeanor showed signs of an extremely kind and motherly nature. She said, "Of course! You can look around and tell me what you like." I was a little shocked, to be quite honest. I found the one! A gorgeous BCBG sequin dress of my dreams! It fit like a glove! Literally, it was really tight and fit like a glove! When she saw me in it, she insisted I *needed* accessories: earrings, bangles, and a Prada coat to match. She styled me beautiful and sent me on my way with all these things, not knowing me from a bucket, and she let me borrow all these gorgeous pieces trusting I would bring them back. All I had prayed for was a dress. I am in tears right now because the goodness of our heavenly Father overwhelms my heart with inexplicable joy. How important is it to look back in our lives and see the footprint of God's goodness? How easily we can forget his faithfulness. Every problem we have is a gorgeous opportunity for exercising our faith. How else would we know who God is if we weren't in situations that required miracles? We already forget his deeds so easily. It's a privilege to go through trials for the sake of learning who God is. The glories of his riches are what our heart was longing for, and in that moment, at Sequels boutique, he showed me there was no need of mine he couldn't provide.

As I returned to give Krista the items, she ended up *giving* me the earrings and the dress as a gift! *What?* I went from not having anything but yoga pants to wear to the ball to having more than what I needed and then some! But do you want to know the most precious thing God gave me from this prayer? It was *Krista's friendship*. She was a light in my very dark world for the next few months. I was deep in healing from the trauma at that time, and she ended up becoming a dear friend of mine and still is. She encouraged me and stood by my side at a very difficult time. This is our God, friends. He is "able to do *immeasurably* more than all we can ask or imagine" (Ephesians 3:20). Sometimes all it takes is looking back and seeing all of the goodness and faithfulness in your life to truly appreciate it for what it is. Gifts and blessings lining our sometimes very painful lives. There is *always* something to be grateful for.

And that wasn't even it. An amazing professional makeup artist agreed to doing my makeup as a gift, and she did a great job. Thank you, Christi Reynolds! Then my friend Leo from my childhood noticed I was doing a red-carpet event (at this point I started back up with social media), and he messaged me and asked if I wanted to get my hair done by his friend who was slaying it with hair and getting his work published in magazines. So I of course said, "Yes, please!!" It was so surreal to me. I went from not having any dreams in my heart anymore to, all of a sudden, everything from my childhood resurrecting. The possibility that the dreams could become a reality both excited me and scared me in a very confusing little package. Everything was starting to work itself out. By prayer and thanksgiving, God provided for me to go from frumpy yoga pant enthusiast- to red-carpet ready!

In the weeks leading up to the premier, as a part of the production team, I knew we had to try different marketing strategies to get the word out about *Splashed*. I was fervent in prayer about it and knew God was going to do a miracle regardless of the outcome; however, sometimes God calls us into action. Faith in action! So I went to Univision (a Spanish TV station) and rang the doorbell to see if I could somehow get an interview on TV. I didn't know at the time where any other television stations were, and I could have Googled it, but I wasn't as resourceful as I am now. I had done a commercial at Univision as a kid. My mom had taken me there when I'd been in high school, so I'd known where the building had been. I sat there pressing the button, praying God would help me pitch this story. Someone answered, I pitched them for about a minute, and they hung up on me. I thought it was a bad connection, so I called back. Again, they hung up on me. A third time, they answered again, and I said something like, "You keep hanging up on me, but I have a good story you might want to hear." I don't remember if it was after the third try or fourth, and I don't want to lie to you, so we'll say that after a few attempts, a producer finally came and opened the door for me. She had me sit in the lobby and tell her why I was there. This was my third or fourth time trying to tell them the story in a five-minute period. Old Libier, *without* God, would have left at the second hang-up, and said, "It didn't happen. Oh well! I knew it wouldn't." She would have walked away, disappointed. *New Libier filled with God-given purpose* knew it wasn't a personal rejection and **kept trying**. I believed in the movie so much and what we were doing, It gave me strength I had never known before. To truly believe in something changed the way I behaved. Although, at that time I still didn't believe in myself. I believed in the collective effort of the cast and the crew, and I was willing to put my pride aside to get the movie the most exposure possible. The producer said yes! After hearing all about the film, she gave us a live, television interview. Wow! My first time on TV, and I was super excited and nervous. To boot, the interview would be in Spanish. I wasn't as comfortable saying all the terms and verbiage about the movie and cause in Spanish. But there I went, having a newfound courage because God's love changed me!

I don't recall right now, but somehow we also got on CBS, on the *Good Day Sacramento Show* and were able to talk about the movie and the premier in English. It was a whirlwind. At that time, I wasn't even really aware of what was happening. My dreams being realized. One thing I can say that I loved learning about through this process was that there will never be a success, dream met, position, "level," or possession that can ever make you feel anything other than what you already feel. Nothing will ever make you feel the way you desire because all these things that we "think" are going to make us fulfilled, happy, worthy, valuable, and peaceful are only by-products of our actions. God wants us to live extraordinary lives, but if we are searching for what only Christ can do for our hearts in something or someone else, we will always feel unfulfilled, and we'll be on to the "next" one. That is why I am 100 percent grateful God did not give me this dream ten years ago. It would have consumed me. I understand that aside from Christ, nothing else matters. When I am filled by him, everything else is a pleasant overflow of what is already filling my spirit with value and worth. I am an empty vessel, and if I don't make the choice to fill myself up with God on a daily basis, the very things that were meant to give me joy and be blessings in my life can become idols I worship, and it closes me off to my heavenly Father's love.

I was going through a very exciting time. We sowed so many prayers, tears, and hard work for the movie, and now, at this season, we were definitely reaping the benefits of our work. But it wasn't what I thought it would be. There was still a feeling of unfulfillment when I had a day in which I didn't submit my heart to God. I have learned that my very purpose is to *worship God in all I do*. Before, I just wanted to be an actress and have that label shout my success. I would say acting was my purpose. I thought once I was successful at that, I would finally feel worthy of love and connection. But if that were to be taken away from me, would I remain without purpose? Would I be valuable if I couldn't be an actor? I was happy to find the answer was yes. My purpose is knowing and believing the love of God. My purpose is relationship with him! I was barely beginning to know who God was for me in that season of my life as I read my Bible. I was overjoyed that all the years I spent thinking I'd be an actress were because he placed that desire there himself. But not to validate me as a person. Not to define me. But for God to shine his glory through me so that I could see it was never about how talented I am but rather to remember whose I am. He placed that desire there so that whatever I chose to do, I could do it to worship the beautiful God who made me. The fulfillment of my soul remains in choosing the love of God on the daily!

16

THE LAND OF THE FREE AND THE HOME OF THE BRAVE

I took a selfie in front of the memorial auditorium where I was celebrating my freedom as a citizen of the United States of America! I became a citizen, guys! I walked in fear of being deported since I came into this country in 1992. The old me would tell younger me to chill out. Everyone thinks I'm American because how *guerita* I am. I tell people I'm Mexican, and they don't believe me. Ha! But I didn't have this peace, unfortunately. I was always in a state of anxiety over not having papers. I felt horrible since my nature was to follow the rules, I hated feeling like that. So when I was able to enjoy my citizenship in November of 2013, I rejoiced with the best of them. So grateful God gave me this amazing opportunity to go from bound to freedom on so many aspects. 2013 was one of the hardest years of my life; however, I grew more in that year than ever. Thank you, America, for all you've provided me with. I love this country and this land. I love the philosophy behind the tapestry of our flag. I am living proof of what the American dream is about. It is not about being given everything; it is about seizing every opportunity and working toward your dreams with faith and hope. And we haven't even started with me actually going toward my dreams. I can't wait for you to finish this book so you can see what happened after God resurrected my dreams! *Splashed* was *only* the beginning. I say this with hope that you would be excited about what God has in store for *you*. My story is just a small reflection of what God does with a life surrendered to him. He can use **anyone** who has a willing heart! He is the King and conqueror of the **impossible**. I was almost a lost cause, and he came and not only redeemed me, but he also gave me life abundant!

Okay, I've made you wait long enough, I'll tell you what happened with our faith of the Crest. On that day in March of 2014, I sat nervously inside the Crest Theatre, looking straight forward at the stage of this beautiful historic place in downtown, Sacramento. The ceiling was plated with gold designs of swirly architecture. My gaze and focus was straight ahead. I had a hot dog and some candy on my lap to enjoy during the movie. I was so nervous; I didn't eat one single bite. That's preposterous. That's how you know something crazy is about to go down. When I am hungry, I *never* refuse food, especially a hot dog and sour patches. Come on, now! As the movie started, I had the case of the nerves, and my palms were so sweaty. I felt as if I were dreaming. After the movie ended, I looked back into that theater, and there sat about seven hundred people. *Seven hundred*! Remember how we needed a max of three hundred to break even? Yep. God is amazing. So many people came to see the work we had done, and for the first time in my life, I understood that God created me with the unique talents and abilities to tell a story for his glory and not my own. He gave me gifts to share, not to hoard for myself. I can allow pride to paralyze me in realizing the highest, most authentic version of myself, or I can push past that resistance every time it comes and honor the God who made me uniquely to act, sing, and perform so I can reflect him and his beauty! God gave us our dreams. He can do abundantly more than what we can think or imagine. Think about that for just a couple of minutes. Sum up all your hopes. Desires. Dreams. Things you giggle about because it seems so audacious and big and huge. "No, it's too farfetched," you say. "It will never happen to me." You sigh. Yeah, God wants to squash that and give you *more*, way, *way*, *more* than that.

"Libier, but you don't know what I've been through," you reply. "You don't understand my situation or all the bad choices I've made in my life. I'm too old. I've failed too many times. I don't have money. I don't have connections. I am not that talented." The list goes on. Beloved, it isn't about your ability or situation; it's about discovering faith to the one who made you **on** purpose, **with** a purpose only *you* can fulfill. Do you think God would make a cheese grater and then tell it to not grate delicious cheese? No! That cheese grater better grate that lactose so I can be gassy as all heavens! The courage to pursue your God-given dreams will always elude you because it's the place where you meet the real you and the maker of your soul. The intersection of: yourself, your dreams, hopes, and desires **with** a loving God who will have your back no matter how many times you fail is hope! And with hope all things can be weathered! Temporary failure is inevitable, but the final victory you have in the bag, beloved. The final victory has been won for you so you aren't aimlessly walking; you are being guided by the God of all creation! He will never leave you, and he will keep you until you die! When you realize the gravity of *you* being *you*, you'll find the courage to move forward with your dreams. It has nothing to do with you. It's all to reflect the living God. There's nothing that can impress him or captivate him more than humility and trust so he will get the glory when you become who *he* created you to be. Listen. We don't deserve what God does, did, and will do for us. We cannot work for it; we cannot repay him. We just have to seek to know him, love him, obey to the best of our ability, and believe and have faith that he is a good, good Father who wants to bless his children. I've never known a love such as that. But it's real. I am living proof. So I believe that IN God we have a land of freedom and can feel at home to **be brave**. Thank you America for the inspiration but I believe this dream is possible not on a physical land but anywhere in the world in the land of your heart with the maker of your soul! You are free to be free and at home to be brave to live life being YOU!

17

TRIGGERS. FREEDOM.

Follow me to the *night* of the premier: March, 7, 2014. A day that would go down in my heart as God's provision and actionable faith made manifest in my life. I got my makeup done by Christi, got my hair did by Ozzie. Put on my dress at my friend Alisa's house, and put my earrings on that Krista gave me. I felt like Cindereya! That's a Mexican version of Cinderella. My great friend Adam used to call me that. It's always stayed with me. I don't remember why Doug wasn't with me at the time of going to the premier, but I was nervous the entire drive with Alisa. I worried about stepping out in faith all those months and wondered if anyone would come and see the movie. What if I got to the Crest and only family members were filling the seats? I pushed back my pessimistic thoughts and just praised God and thanked him for all he had *already* done. I was experiencing something I had been dreaming about ever since I'd been a tiny, little girl. Let alone the fact that this happened supernaturally. I never had to "seek" it. I didn't manipulate *anyone* into giving me the part or the makeup or the dress. I didn't hustle to get to where God had placed me. I didn't have to compromise my dignity or give any part of my body for any of these things. My integrity and my character had been preserved. I had a family. A husband and two children. God so lovingly wove this into my destiny that it didn't take an unhealthy toll on my life or family. Yes, there were struggles, because it's life, and there are always struggles. But God's grace and favor was upon this season and chapter in my life so intensely that I felt his presence for the first time in my life. I finally felt the presence and love of God. For so long I had heard about his love. I heard about him and maybe believed him for others. But I had never experienced it for *myself.* All it took was surrendering my life and dreams to him. It was as if he said, "Okay, my lovely child, you have chosen me and my will. You've stopped trying to do it all by yourself, and now I'm going to knock your socks *off.* Watch what I can do!" For so long, I had tried to make this dream my reality, and it had never worked. Because I'd been going at it alone. I'd been doing it on my timeline. My terms. For *my* glory. I was never meant to do it by myself, and it was never meant to consume me in pride. He had placed the desire there for *his* will and glory to shine so that I could meet him and know him and believe he is God.

When Alisa and I parked in the garage, I could feel my heart in my throat. We walked up to the Crest. The Crest is on K Street, a very cool street in the downtown part of Sacramento, nestled between urban and wilderness parts. There is always a lot of action on that street because it's home to many bars and restaurants. It's also home to a lot of people. It's always interesting being on that street; you never know the adventures you'll have. A lively place, I will say! You find all sorts of adventure! As I walked up, I saw the lights that livened the Crest's sign, and my heart ticked a tiny bit faster. When we turned right to walk on K, I saw what my eyes will remember as a miracle for the rest of my life. A red carpet and the marquee with the name of the movie I starred in, which shot on zero budget and a whole lot of people. A line that, to my eyes, had no end! Whoa! I'm not very good at counting people at events! Just ask Doug.

When we go to sporting events, he'll ask me, "How many people do you think are at Dodger Stadium right now?" I'll say, "Probably like five hundred?" He looks at me in disbelief and tells me the real number, and I about fall off my chair! I'm completely okay with not knowing that kind of stuff. My mind isn't made to calculate people. My mind is preoccupied with what outfit I'm going to wear and how the textures are going to complement each other, okay? Okay! Anyway, with that said, my mind just saw a lot of people. And my jaw dropped. We were hoping for three hundred or more to break even, remember? Well, about seven hundred people showed up at the Crest that amazing night! Are you freakin' kidding me? That's amazing! People wanted pictures with me. There was a red-carpet interview. Honestly, things that I dreamt about as a kid. God is amazing. I "took delight in the Lord and he gave me the desires of my heart" (Psalm 37:4). He is a good Father. That's the point of the story!

Here ends the exciting/fun news for a little while. That night was amazing. I will rejoice in it for my entire life. Seeing God's faithfulness filled me up with his love and 100 percent certainty that he **was** my Father, and that he **was** for me, which was what I needed for what happened in my life *next*.

Please prayerfully read the next section so your heart will be guarded from any traumatic triggers.

The night of the premier, I heard a gal's story of being sold into human trafficking since she was an itty, bitty girl by her family. It *hurt* my heart so much to hear her story. She spoke about God giving her hope, and that made me glad, but I was so *angry* after hearing the devastating events that happened to her. It made me sick to my stomach, and I asked God why I was so angry and what he wanted me to do about with my anger! I felt the answer right away. I wanted to help anyone who had been exploited and sexually abused. At this point in my life, on March 7, 2014, I knew I had been abused and shown pornography but I had no actual memory of any details of anything more. I knew something was off obviously from all that I was struggling with. I knew because of the promiscuity in my life as a kid. I knew because I felt shame. I knew because I cut myself. I knew because I had so much self-hatred. I knew **something** was off. I knew that something happened to me; I just didn't know what. And after the premier and hearing her story, I was dealing with intense emotional pain I hadn't dealt with, **ever**. I was so far from feeling like myself. I could no longer pretend everything was fine. I was so angry. I am not suggesting that anyone who struggles with these things has been sexually abused, but I am suggesting that you don't feel you're weird for the pain you feel inside from whatever hurt has been caused in your heart. I believe we all have a story. I am suggesting we all need a big dose of healing from *whatever* disappointment, trauma, or hurt in our lives that is hindering us from knowing God more intimately. Healing for the sake of living the lives God has for us. I believe we cannot live the life God has for us unless we face the deep wounds that have been infected in our souls. He wants to heal you from whatever it is that has harmed you in *any* way! I desired God to heal me, but I didn't know what it was or whom I should be working toward forgiving.

Days after the premier, I was deep in prayer about human trafficking, and I kept thinking, *God, I know I was hurt, however that was, but it doesn't compare to what* **those** *kiddos go through. I had never been exploited and abused like* **that**. In the depths of my soul, God showed me I had been hurt, and it mattered to him just the same to heal me, as it did to heal others with *different* wounds. I kept comparing my circumstances to that of others who had it "worse" because I didn't know how to have compassion for my own story. I didn't understand these were painful instances that hindered me from living life abundantly. I was so bound to shame, fear, and worthlessness because of all I had been through, and I was willing to go help others but not *myself*. God told me before I could help anyone else: he first had to help me. He had to heal me.

The morning right after my prayer for healing and resolution to my anger, I remembered shattering details of my abuse. On March 7, 2013 God gave me the memories of my childhood abuse. All the details I needed at that time to enter into the most difficult and most emotionally painful season of my life. I felt a pain so deep, I couldn't even physically walk. I had just ex-perienced some of the best feelings in my life: having a beautiful family and realizing my dreams, and then it was as if *everything* came crashing down. All of a sudden, I didn't care about anyone or anything. Not even myself. But I knew courage was necessary to walk into this healing time with God. I knew he was calling me into the wilderness, and I wanted to obey. In prayer I asked God to cover my family with his grace from my raw heart and attitude. I now believe that the Holy Spirit was the one guiding me in that prayer. I had no clue what was about to go down.

The last thing I want to do is exalt my pain over the goodness and faithfulness of God. Even though this was an excruciatingly painful season of my life, God gave me hope and joy. On days when I didn't know if I would make it, he carried me in his strength. It was a miracle that I was finally able to process all of my feelings from being abused. I was no longer trying to hold it in or reject the pain. I just let it be. In so many ways, I felt freedom I've never had in my life experienced. My eyes hurt from crying, but I felt God cleansing me with every tear. He showed me that it was not my fault. That I, no matter how my body responded, didn't seek the abuse, in *any* way. He showed me my innocence through my little girl, whom at the time, was four. That was the age I began being molested. I was forced by a neighbor to watch pornography. Can you imagine? At that age, do you think anyone is capable of knowing whether it is right or wrong to watch that? I finally understood my brokenness and why I had such a stronghold to it as an adult. It was a lifestyle for me that had seemed *normal*. Until God came and broke those chains and set me free. But to begin, I had to take action. I was forced to watch at an age where I could not defend myself. However, I was now an adult and had the responsibility to take action. I knew that my sin came from a broken place and finally realized God understood why I did what I did.

That he was interested in first showing me who he was and how much he loved me. Then he was interested in healing the broken parts that prevented me from receiving him because of how much shame and guilt I felt. Then he wanted to gift me with obedience to change and to be the strength in my weakness. He wanted to change me so he could use me for his kingdom, so anyone else struggling with similar shame and fear and worthlessness could see that he could love them, just as he loved me to health. I am nothing "special;" if he can work miracles in me, no one is too far gone. Trust me, if I could have driven him away, I would have.

I fell into sin so many times. I stumbled so many times. It was war against sin, and I failed time and time again. But he wasn't interested in my failures; he was interested in showing himself as faithful and as my God my savior! When you're put in a place that is beyond your strength and human frailty, and God pulls you out with his loving Word, you believe *him at* his Word. If I could have done it in my own strength, I would not appreciate God's grace over my life. I had to be at the end of my rope to truly believe in him. I was such a skeptic. He proved to me, time and time again, he was God in this painful season. I would not be here to write these words to you now if it weren't for his relentless pursuit of my heart. I am weeping with gratitude and in awe of how far we've come, hoping this book will help anyone who feels broken beyond repair so he or she can have hope for the future! God can work miracles, especially when a life and heart are surrendered to his love! For the longest time, I felt disgusting and filled with shame. Like no one in their right mind would truly love me if they saw who I *really* was. I had it so wrong. Abuse has a way of twisting an innocent brain into thinking you're the reason why it happened. God showed me I couldn't hide from him as I could from people. He always saw the darkest places in my soul, but as I finally invited him in, he began his miraculous work of changing them with the truth. I experienced a precious intimacy that was beyond anything else I had ever known. The intoxicating presence of Jesus that made me believe even through this pain I was going to be okay. There was hope for my life. That he died so I could live.

In the intimate moments I had with him in truth—sitting in my closet reading my Bible, weeping for believing my innocence wasn't taken—I would hold my Bible to my chest as a way of saying, "Get in here. Get in here so I can feel differently." And there my passion for reading the Word of God caught fire. Who knew that what my soul longed for all along was with me all along. I just didn't have the eyes to see him; they were clouded with shame that didn't belong to me. In those moments of intense grief, I felt truly known, *all of me*. Truly loved, *all of me*. Truly accepted, *all of me*. Fully known and unconditionally loved in my mess, as is. He loved me deeply in the dark and helped me see I could chose differently when I felt his unconditional love. Because I felt loved, I wanted to be better. It wasn't the other way around. I didn't have to wait until I got my shit together to be loved. Excuse and pardon my French, sometimes a well-placed "ish" is better than any other word. I realized that I didn't have to pretend to be a "good Christian." I didn't have to pretend to have everything together. I could stop pretending and just be me. It felt like a freedom I had never known—a truly satisfying place to be: in the arms of Jesus, free to be me.

I used to be that girl who was always happy. I probably annoyed some folks because I tried my very best to always be in a good mood. This worked when the pressures of life weren't so severe. But when I was in this healing mode, with a husband and two kiddos who depended deeply on me, my mood was all over the place. I felt embarrassed that I couldn't keep it together. I was fighting with an old way of being and finally being in agreement with my soul. Finally I felt all the pain I never allowed to come forward. I know there is power in positive thoughts. I have seen miraculous change in my life because of the thoughts I feed my brain. But when you're denying your pain, your not being honest and it can really be harmful. Clean pain is necessary for our human condition. Allowing all emotions God gave us and not denying what we feel is a freedom and privilege not many get to experience. God can handle all our emotions and he wont' turn you down. He'll listen and comfort and temper anything you bring to him. Best of all, he will counsel you in the way you should move forward.

I believe if you have not faced trauma and dealt with it and sat with the uncomfortable feelings that surge when you are face to face with what has hurt your heart, it can be detrimental to your life. You'll always be secretly bound to the fear of your wounds. Your heart will lie to you and say that it can't handle that much pain, it honestly just doesn't want to. You can and will handle it, if you walk into it with God. God will hold all things together. For an entire year, I pretty much cried every day. I had anxiety up the wazoo and dealt severely with PTSD. Scary PTSD that made me believe my husband was going to rape me or hurt me, and I was scared to have to defend myself. You have no idea the depths of hell our family went through in this time. I was finally letting go, and my feelings were consuming, until they were not.

God always rescued me from a panic attack. I allowed acceptance to be the backbone of my healing, and when the panic came, I embraced the ride. I stopped rejecting my big emotions After a few PTSD moments in prayer, God showed me this was my soul's way of mourning and grieving what I endured. This was my soul releasing toxic pent up emotions that, mask as I tried, came out to bite me when I least expected it. At least in this way I was in a controlled environment. Through prayer, I would just sit in a dark room where no one could hear me and let go. The poison slowly but surely seeped out of my heart. The bitterness and resentment that made me blow up at my littles or my husband, who had no part in my abuse, was finally allowed to make its way out and not on them. I messed up many times and blew up at my husband and kids. That's when God's grace washed over our home. I hope one day my littles can see that any of my issues were never because of them. That Mommy was just going through a lot of pain and seeking her mental health and freedom in Christ. It was messy. It still sometimes is. Healing won't be overnight but it's gotten so much richer because I know after each wave of healing I'll be more of who God created me to be I will be even that much more free.

A year of healing seemed like it would never end. It took a long while of intense healing. I mean that's all I focused on. A year seems long, especially when you're in the trenches of recovery and healing. I'll tell you the truth though: I would do it again. I have gained so much from healing! There is healing in the pain. God will always give you beauty for ashes. He assured me in the dark that he would pay me double in joy what I endured in pain. My suffering wasn't in vain. He took what the devil meant for evil and used it for my good and the good of many around me. That seemed like a pretty good deal to me! If I could go through this suffering knowing that God was somehow going to do something beautiful from it, that it would help someone who had been hurt like me, I would go through it everything time and time again. I heard this beautiful quote by Viktor Frankl in my time of healing. "In some ways, suffering ceases to suffering at the moment it finds a meaning, such as the meaning of a sacrifice." Here's the song I wrote out of the darkest season of my life.

New

Verse 1:

In a world that's dark and lonely

When the odds were stacked against her

When they yelled out that she's nothing

And she's become someone's pleasure

Verse 2:

She might be badly wounded

Her heart might feel destroyed

She's got angst in her stomach

Confusion in her head

Chorus

If you can brave it, then you will make it

You will make it through, you will make it through

Don't lose your hope

Trade in for beauty instead of ashes

Verse 3:

In the midst of broken places

She's been made new

Nothing rips her apart from real love

Every tear has been recorded

There's been healing through the pain

She can finally hold her head up without shame

You are made new. Everything is new.

New. Everything is new.

New. Everything is new.

You are made new

There's a purpose in your future more important than the past

Trade it for beauty instead of ashes.

18

FINDING TREASURE

I came out victorious over many enslavements as I endured the pain of heal-ing. I want you to truly know that I still struggle with certain things. I am not perfect in these areas at all whatsoever; they just don't hold me captive any-more from living the life God has for me. I can confidently push forward, and I recognize them in me faster now when I'm struggling in any of these areas). These victories include the following.

Freedom from anger

Freedom from fear

Freedom from performance-based love

Freedom from thinking I was damaged and not worthy of love and connection

Freedom from a victim mentality: I believe it is absolutely necessary to go through the pain of healing when you are a victim of abuse, and you will feel like a victim because you were. However, God won't let you stay there. He will restore you until you don't feel like a victim of anything anymore. You will feel like more than a conqueror, victorious! A royal princess or prince with an inheritance of love, peace, hope, and life abundant in Jesus Christ!

Freedom from eating disorders, self-harm, and excessive working out

Freedom from placing my value anywhere else other than God: I used to place my worth and value in my sexual appeal, outer appearance, the labels of the clothes I wore, the number on the scale, how much worldly success I had (how many "likes" on my pictures; how many followers on my Instagram; who laughed at my jokes; other people's opinions about me). I also placed my value and worth in not making mistakes, having a well put-together life, and my children's behavior.

Freedom from always expecting so much of myself and others

Freedom from perfectionism and controlling behavior

Freedom from depression and anxiety

Freedom from skepticism and a worst-case-scenario mentality

Freedom from an orphan spirit

Freedom from abusive tendencies

Freedom from addiction (to all things that made me numb the pain)

Freedom from comparison and envy

Freedom from toxic thoughts and relationships

Freedom from believing I was alone in this world, that no one understood me or was in my court

Freedom from codependency and feeling responsible for placating others

Freedom from hopelessness

I finally understood the following.

I was loved beyond my wildest imagination (1 Corinthians 13).

I had a huge inheritance in Christ, and I could claim it (Psalm 2: 7–8).

God made me who I am specifically for a purpose only I can fulfill (Exodus 9:16).

I could allow me to be me (Psalm 139:14).

Others' opinions about me were just that: their opinions. I didn't have to believe it. I could choose to believe God's truth above any person whose breath was in their nostrils (Isaiah 2:2).

I was a threat to the devil: I had a target on my back, so I was going to have to fight strategically (with God's Word) to enter into my calling (Ephesians 6:12).

I will never experience anything that God can't use for my good (Romans 8:28).

I had support from God (2 Chronicles 16:9).

I had the freedom to choose what I wanted to do, and God would delight in helping me learn from it: whatever I chose, there he'd be. This one always tripped me up, especially as a young Christian. I would always worry that I wasn't going to pick the right thing, and in all honesty, I felt afraid that I would lose God's love through wrong choices. Now I understand that God will never leave me; he will never forsake me (Deuteronomy 31:6). No matter what I end up choosing, even if it's the "wrong" choice when my heart is full of repentance, gratitude, and prayer—giving anything to him—he will turn the situation around into a blessing. There's no place we can flee from him. Trust me, if I could have driven him away, I would have with my rebellion, skepticism, and the habitual sin that dampened my life. He is so patient and kind and loves us deeply. He will never let you go!

Faith means everything to God (Hebrews 11:6).

My faith doesn't depend on me; he hooks me up large when I ask (Hebrews 12:2).

Sin is anything, anything that separates us from his love: see, I used to be so scared of the word "sin." God showed me not to be scared of it. He showed me not to fail to recognize it as well. When I realized that he was a good father, the word "sin" took a different tone in my heart. I understood him wanting to help me and that what he called sin in my life was a choice I made that was a cheap substitute for the fragrant and fulfilling love he could give me. I'll give you an example. When I used to smoke a pack of cigarettes a day, I felt mad that God wanted to take that from me. I felt as if it were my "one" thing that I delighted in. I felt I was treating myself in some way. I didn't want to give up something I enjoyed. My husband hated it, and somehow it made me want to do it even more, ha! Rebellion at its best. No one is gonna tell me what to do. I'll smoke myself silly if I want to! Anyway, God showed me that I was trying to numb my feelings. My anxiety was something he wanted to heal forever and not just put a Band-Aid over. He showed me that by my obedience to treating my body kindly and quitting I was actually recognizing that he made this body for me, that I was his work of art. He showed me that as I pruned the habitual sin from my life, his intense love, which surpasses my comprehension, would fill me up so much, and it would not be a ten-minute "cigarette break" that would appease my anxious soul; rather, it was his loving light shining in my heart that would placate any fear or anxiety, and it would not be so fleeting. He has always been the desire of my soul, I just never knew how satisfying his love would be until I decided to give it a sober shot. I would never trade what I feel for another vice. His love is so deep. I say this with so much trepidation because I have an addictive personality, and sometimes I feel afraid that I will go back, but I have to trust that one day at a time surrendered to him will prevent that from happening. One day at a time.

Everyone is sinful and falls short of the glory of God: everyone has something he or she needs forgiveness from, errrrry day, not one is good (Romans 3:10). Don't let your aunt, Pachoully, make you believe that because she doesn't kill anybody, she's better than folks. Or let yourself fall into the trap that you have no sin to repent of. Trust me, when you become honest with yourself about that, God can finally start working on you, so that you might know him and receive him better. Trust me, I was the queen of saying I was a good person. No. I. Am. Not. More on our depravity in the next chapter. Don't be too excited! No, but honestly, this was a huge revelation for me. I regularly struggled with pride. So I often either felt better than someone or worse than someone. If I looked up to someone, I would all of the sudden put them up on a pedestal and think of them as a saint. It was a disservice to me and them because one, he or she had a greater chance of disappointing me when he or she didn't live up to his or her "idol" status. Or two, I felt someone was way worse than me because I wasn't "messing" up as he or she was. It was sort of a way to make me feel better about myself because my confidence wasn't in my savior, rather in my behavior.

On November 12, 2014, I was going through one of the most excruciatingly painful times of my life. It had been a very difficult season in my life and my family's lives as well. When momma ain't happy, ain't nobody happy. That has been a true and tried motto in this house. I'd asked that God's grace would cover much of the crazy mood swings I had been having, and I'd known that his grace had covered so much of my shortcomings that past year.

I was going through a healing time with God. He had called me to the Wilderness with him, and we were sitting in a very dark, very painful, and uncomfortable place, he and I. Before I started reading my Bible a lot more consistently, I didn't know there was much of my life that needed to be changed. I think I'd been living in a safe reality that I had so carefully created for myself. I was safe. I pretended to myself that I was "content" with my place in life, and I wasn't going to take many risks. As long as my little world spun my way, I was fine. I did so much to try to control my life—and that of my husband and kids—in order to not feel out of control. But to be honest, it was getting to be too exhausting, and I could tell something was wrong. I just couldn't tell you what the heck the matter was. I was trying to fix things as they popped up instead of going to the root of my issues.

I knew before I started reading my Bible that I had many flaws. I knew that. But I didn't know that God wanted to help me shed some of the things that were hindering me from knowing him better and from living a life full of adventure, joy, and peace. Freedom was something I thought I had, until then. I knew God was setting me free in those moments. It wasn't until I was honest with myself and with God about the state of my heart that the healing began. I didn't trust God. I wasn't free, and I didn't show many signs of the fruit of his spirit. I knew I was being a hypocrite calling myself a Christian when the life I led pointed the opposite direction.

As I healed, God kept helping me understand each step when I was ready. I remember being at the stage of acceptance. I prayed for God to help me have acceptance as the backbone of my healing. When I first learned that I had been sexually abused, I didn't want to believe the little girl inside me telling me there was something wrong. God exposed all the truth so it would set me free. It had been the most painful thing I'd ever felt as a thirty-year-old woman to admit to myself that I had been badly hurt. But in accepting it, I have been able to experience peace. I have been able to understand myself a little deeper and to know that it was not my fault. I no longer feel angry all the time. God has allowed me to process my emotions in his loving arms. I struggled with anxiety, and I'd had more panic attacks than I'd like to admit. But through every one, the minute I allowed it to just be, the minute I surrendered all of my emotions to God; it was as if black tar was flowing from my heart outward into his light and being changed into good energy instead of being stuck inside of me and coming out at non-welcomed times and places. I knew that if I didn't decide to heal with God on this, it would eventually kill me. If it didn't kill me physically it would have mentally and emotionally.

That is why I trusted God to help me heal. But with healing came pain. I had been so badly hurt in my life that I was terrified of pain. The more I healed, the more accepting of pain I became. I welcomed it because I would rather be in pain and know peace and my savior than pretend nothing was wrong, feeling hopeless, bitter, and angry. There was healing in the pain. There was an end to the madness. My pain became energy to help someone else with their pain, and my hope was that their pain would help someone else with their pain, and so on and so forth. I have learned that all of the things that happened to me have the opportunity to work for the good of me and other people.

In Genesis 50:20, Joseph said to his brothers, "You intended to hurt me but God intended it for good to accomplish what is now being done, the saving of many lives." I know that this is hard stuff to hear and to talk about. But the devil loves secrecy for that very reason. It isolates us and makes us feel as if we're the only damaged one. That is a lie from the pit of hell!

God has such a loving and compassionate heart. He knows what we all have been through, and he wants to heal us from all of our pain. In this life, my pain may never go away completely. I know I will remember the feeling I had when I started to heal so I can empathize with another sister or brother of mine who has gone through the same thing. I can hold them tightly and tell them of how God has redeemed me and that he will do the same for them. I actually don't want to forget. The people who have helped me the most in this trying time have been people who have also suffered pain and know how to give an encouraging hug and point me to Jesus. We will never have the ability to heal anyone in our lives. We have to realize him or her into the hands of Jesus. But what we can do is what the Bible instructs us to do, which is to "mourn with those who mourn; rejoice with those who rejoice" (Romans 12:15).

I may have been in pain then, but I was recovering. The one thing I wouldn't do was give up. I heard Christine Caine say this, and I could not agree more: "The devil on his best day didn't take me out on my worst day." God has already won the fight. We need only to grasp his hand tightly and let him help us embrace the pain of recovery. Because the devil will tell you that because you're in pain you are still not healed. No, friends! It's because we are healing that we feel pain. Praise God.

By allowing God to help me heal, the quality and amazingness of my life have doubled! I can now hold my head up high with the dignity God provides me. I do believe that in heaven I will not experience any of this pain. And you won't either.

19

DEPRAVITY

My depravity. That sounds so bad! No one wants to go here or think about his or her own depravity. Can you just picture me saying this with a really scary, deep, and intimidating voice? Yes, me too. I am the type of person who can't put it on the shelf when I learn something. I feel like a mind detective, and I am fascinated by our brains. I've always been so interested in understanding how the human mind works. I would say I would play one heck of a movie detective, side note! Not quite sure how I'd do at really being one in real life though. Most of the time when my husband shaves, I can't tell until hours and hours have gone by! Not the point. Getting back on track here. My husband and I go to Forest Home, and it's a Christian family camp we love. One year, one of the messages the entire week was on depravity. Let's read the definition:

de-prav-i-ty (noun). dəˈpravədē/ (deep scary voice): moral corruption; wickedness. "A tale of wickedness and depravity." Synonyms: corruption, vice, perversion, deviance, degeneracy, immorality, debauchery, dissipation, profligacy, licentiousness, lechery, prurience, obscenity, indecency; et cetera.

A wicked or morally corrupt act. Christian theology: the innate corruption of human nature, due to original sin.

Akk. I don't want to view myself like this, ya feel me? I don't want to admit I am lechery. Mmm, that kind of sounds like "milk" in Spanish. Maybe for my husband's sake, I do want to be lechery. He loves leche. No! I don't want to be wicked or morally corrupt. But I am. It doesn't matter the kind of sin I struggle with. It could be one that is seen, such as alcoholism or gluttony. Or one that is hidden in the deepest part of my souls, such as pride and unbelief. If I keep treating myself as not guilty in this matter, I will completely lose out on what God has for me when I repent of whatever sin is encroaching my soul. There is freedom in surrendering and in putting all our dirty laundry into the light. The light is what will heal it. First of all, you can't hide anything from God. Brother, he knows what you think when you see that attractive girl and your wife is sitting right next to you. Sister, he knows that you profess to know him to make yourself liked by your Bible study hermanas, but secretly you don't really know or have not experienced the gospel the way Jesus intended you to. He knows all that plagues us; we can't hide our ickiness from him. However, he won't touch what isn't brought to light. He loves and respects us too much to inflict on our free will. If we aren't the ones initiating the healing process, he will respectfully allow us to exert our will. I'm presuming it hurts God to watch us live our lives so far from his love, all because of all the guilt we feel from the depravity that darkens our spiritual self. I think the devil would love nothing more than for you and I to remain the same. If you aren't rocking the boat, neither will he. If he sees you tripping yourself up, why bother with you? It's when you start going to God with your issues that all hell will break loose. You'll feel as if you're drowning until you're not. Until you're in a place with clear water springs, living a life so full of peace and joy you never imagined. There's a reason to fight for living free of habitual sin! The minute you taste God's goodness, you won't want to go back. It's as if you're living for the first time in your life, and you feel freedom and hope you've never felt before. But you have to bring any dark places in your heart to the light. You can't heal yourself! Time won't do it either! It has to be the Lord himself! Sometimes we can't see what is holding us back. But I am a firm believer that if we ask God to reveal to us the areas that are keeping us from him, he will be more than willing to help! He loves you so stinkin' much. He doesn't want you to feel alone, scared, depressed, anxious, fearful, doubtful, angry, resentful, tired, hopeless, burned out, et cetera. "He came that you would have life, and life abundant" (John 10:10). But the devil is here to destroy us, to steal our hope, to kill our joy, and to rob us of the goodness of repentance, surrender, and belief in God! So in our depravity, the best thing we can do is repent, and in faith receive that precious love, mercy, and forgiveness Christ died for, that we would experience it every day. Jesus died so you and I would be justified (as if we'd never sinned). Are you kidding me? that's an amazing gift that doesn't make sense. We don't deserve it. We can never pay it back, yet it's available to anyone who believes! "This righteousness is given through faith in Jesus Christ to all who believe" (Romans 3:22).

20

EGO- EGO -MY BIGG'OL, EGO!

In the months after the Premier of Splashed, we got accepted to be in two film festivals, the Sacramento one—which we got disqualified from because we had already premiered the movie beforehand—and AOF, Action On Film in Monrovia, CA. We were sad about the Sacramento festival but also knew it was just meant to go down as it did. So we put our focus into being prepared and going to AOF. I was so delighted to get to hop on a plane and go to Monrovia and see our "little movie that could" premier on a screen there. I also got word that I got nominated for an award! Best Actress in a Feature. I was one of five nominees, and there were a ridiculous amount of movies entered. I don't say this to boast in myself. Honestly, without God, my skill is nothing; it is a gift he has given me. I know that now, but back then, my talent was clouded in fear of not being good enough. Pride encroached every aspect of my ability and, honest to goodness, I didn't believe myself to be beautiful or talented. I thought I just had this eminent desire to be an actress, but I didn't believe I had the chops to make it happen. In that time, I was so susceptible to being swayed by people's opinions, so much so that if someone said an unkind word to me, it would affect me to my core! I felt so unworthy of the call God had placed in my life until I experienced Splashed. Until I surrendered it to God and let him lead me. When I gave up my life for Jesus, I found it tenfold. It was no longer this thing that I had to do to be of value. It was more like there was value in me from Jesus loving me, and I desperately wanted to share the gift he gave me with others.

Come with me to a moment before Splashed even happened. Before, when I still felt creatively dead and frustrated. It was truly a moment that changed my life, forever. Erik Thoennes, a teacher from Biola University, was the speaker one year at Forest Home, one day at camp he sat by me at lunch and we chatted. I liked him just fine. I found him to be a great teacher and awesome speaker, despite the difficult message he was delivering. As we were lunching, we struck up a casual conversation, and I was sharing how much I loved acting, but told him singing was scary for me because I was afraid I didn't do it well. Something like that. I didn't know if I was good enough. I vividly remember his response. He looked at me and said, "You know, I hate it when artists are so egotistical that they can't get over themselves and just do what God called them to do." I can't say this is an "accurate quote," but that's how it stuck with me. I felt a little offended at first, but later, in prayer, I explored what this meant for me, and I became so grateful for Erik's truth bomb! He did the most loving thing toward me; he spoke the truth in love. You ever notice how when we get handed a mouthful of truth, it stings? Yep. I didn't want to believe it. I just hadn't really heard of such a concept as frankly as Erik so lovingly gifted me. I meditated upon it, I started a discussion with God about it. I asked if I was being an egomaniac with my feelings of doubt and fear of not being good enough to share my art. Well God said yep. He taught me that pride prevents so many artists from finding their full expression because they are under the very wrong assumption that they are the ones whose talent depends upon. God is the source of our talent, and when we go to him for inspiration, it cannot run out because God is infinitely creative. But we artists tend to think that our art is ours. So we do all sorts of weird things with it. We hoard it. We doubt it. We curse it. We exalt it over God. We take credit for it. We exploit it. We throw it away. We hide it. We ridicule it. We enjoy it. According to Oxford Dictionaries, the following is a definition for "art."

ärt/ noun: the expression or application of human creative skill and imagination, typically in a visual form such as painting or sculpture, producing works to be appreciated primarily for their beauty or emotional power. Art, as I know it, is what God has used my entire life to raise me, comfort me, inspire me, make me giggle, help me run faster, dance harder, and heal me from trauma. God has used the expression of a courageous soul using skill and imagination to guide me on my journey of life. The art of others has influenced who I am today. I would love to high-five every artist who was so bold and courageous to put themselves out there for my sake. Thank you! It's not easy making art. It's easy to criticize it. Not easy making it. As artists, we count the cost of looking like a fool, in any way, and take note of the pain our hearts are not willing to suffer if our art is misunderstood or dismissed. It hurts to create authentic art because it is an expression of who that person is, and if it's rejected? It could seem like rejection to the very core. Painful! However, if you don't try, there's nothing to risk. The full expression of artists is seeing what God can do through our weakness and imperfection. Because then it becomes relevant; then it becomes a source of healing for the artist and others, as well. When the artist is rooted and grounded in the love of God, he or she can grasp his or her value beyond who likes his or her art or who doesn't. When the artist's cup is full by God's measure, he or she has the freedom to create art that isn't subject to a person's ridicule. The person can have their opinion about the art and artist without the artist feeling less than. As an artist this is the epitome of artistic freedom! Delighting in the abundance that comes from surrendering to the first artist who created you and I as a gorgeous expression of his image!

God turned this concept of talent upside down for me. The first thing I realized was I was made with the purpose for a purpose. Secondly, I had the gifts and abilities I did for my purpose; it wasn't happenstance. Those gifts and abilities are irrevocable (Romans 11:29), and it was going to be for God's glory that he was going to use them and bless others and me, through those abilities and gifts, so that I and others would know he is God almighty. I had tried to be an artist for many, many years by myself. Then I'd tried it with God, and the experiences had been polarizing. It became about something different than proving to myself and others that I was worthy of love and acceptance. It became about doing all unto God for the sake of thanking him for making me who I am, for saving me from the pit of hell, and for giving me gifts to delight in. I didn't win the award for Best Actress that night in Monrovia. But what I did win was a sense of who I was, and that was the best award this girl could have ever asked for. To know and pursue the notion that I wasn't in competition with anyone else. I didn't have to strive to be. I could just remain still, and let the love of God lavish my soul and have no doubt that he would place opportunity in my way as he saw fit. All I had to do was press into him, and he'd guide me. It hasn't been easy. No, it's been possible because of who God was. He would knock your socks off if you let him. There's a great adventure awaiting anyone who'd be so bold to believe. To get to experience the partnership of relationship with your Father in heaven in the process of becoming the highest most authentic version of yourself.

You've got to fall in love with the process. You've got to fall in love with your maker and know that even when you fail on your journey, God has your victory! When my name was not called by the announcer of awards at AOF, I felt the pain of rejection surging through my veins. It did sting. It did hurt. I was disappointed. It would have been cool to say I'd won the award for Best Actress in a Feature. However, I knew that wasn't my award. My loss became more meaningful. God showed me the miracles that were taking place in my heart. For the first time in my life, as I faced rejection, I treated myself differently. I wasn't offended to the core. I didn't see it as a personal rejection. My inner dialogue wasn't rude and unkind, as it would have been before. The loss of the title didn't discourage me so much that I didn't want to pursue the next adventure. I was genuinely happy for the woman who won. I even congratulated her in the bathroom. That's a miracle because I had never felt that way in my entire life. To be happy for another human who just got what you wanted. That's a changed heart if I ever saw one! I felt abundant and grateful for the experience and not jaded an defeated. True, lasting change was taking place.

As we sat around the tables of the gala, we heard the speeches from the people winning the awards. Then a famous actress won an award for being in the entertainment industry for many years. She, with the help of her son, slowly made her way up the stage and charmed the audience with her witty speech. Everyone cheered and clapped for her. I was delighted to have been able to experience that! It left me excited for this new phase of my life. Was I going to resurrect the old dream bank and fully pursue an acting career in Sacramento married with children? I didn't know, but I was definitely inspired. As my friend Sara and I were heading out a tad early from the event, we noticed the actress and her son coming out early as well. We did what any fan would do and headed over to talk to her. I told her how much her speech had moved me, but she didn't even look me in the eye. She just said to her son that she needed to use the bathroom. Her son looked a little lost, so Sara and I suggested we could take her to the nearest ladies' room.

They said yes, so here I was holding this woman's arm to escort her to the potty. She had a completely different demeanor off stage than from her vibrant speech. She was tired and sick, and I believe from what I saw, she just wanted to go home and rest. Her tummy was sick. I was a little confused. But it made me realize that we often glamorize the dreams we dream. Or people we admire. In the end, people are still people. Flawed and fragile, with a guaranteed expiration date. At the end of the day, we all need to poop. And

I'll tell you something, the day that diarrhea plagues your little behind, nothing else matters. No achievement, no nothing. Try as we might to add value to ourselves through different means, we will not succeed. It's futile. So sad because we are blinded to the fact that we are of value already. Nothing can add to it. Nothing can subtract from it. So believe in yourself, beloved friend. Do it because God called you to so you can express the very essence of your being into something that cannot be explained other than by your precious art! Some will get it, some will not. It doesn't matter. Someone's waiting, just for you.

21

DREAM BABY, DREAM!

There's not one person who is more together than the other. We all have the same worth, no matter what we've achieved. The Monrovia experience of "dating" Hollywood in God's protection, so to speak, taught me to proceed my dream quest with caution, for the heart can be deceiving sometimes. It wants what it wants until it's brought to submission to the one who created it. God will either give you the desires of your heart if you press into him and live a life that is pleasing to him, or he will change your desires to what he desires for you (which, in my experience, has been way better than what I would have imagined!). And you know what? I don't exactly know what living a life that is pleasing to him means exactly. I just do the best I can and ask for forgiveness when I mess up. Grace is my pace! Most times, I feel as though I take two steps forward, twenty-seven steps back. Sometimes I think I am the least qualified person to do anything of value. I don't have a college degree. I'm an immigrant woman with no paycheck to "validate me." I fail miserably on a weekly basis. I make a ton of mistakes. Yet my heart is wildly in love with Jesus and what he's done for me, so I press into him as if my life depends on it. I'm understanding that my journey isn't going to be perfect. Only God is perfect.

God isn't thinking, If you get all the answers right and don't make any mistakes, then I'll love you and bless you. I believe he is actually counting on us royally messing up. I believe from my very limited knowledge that God just wants us to believe him (as much as we can at any given time) and pursue him and have a relationship with him; everything else just starts falling into place from there. If he gives you the desires of your heart, it will be amazing, and if he decides to change a dream in your heart to look different, it will also be great. Listen, he is the biggest desire of our souls. When we have his love and a holy relationship with him through his Word, we can enjoy peace. Peace will surpass all our understanding, and the love of Christ will be the thing that makes us whole and successful. In my experience, this choice has to be made daily. I choose him daily, sometimes, in my case, even hourly.

I get so scared to make him so upset with my failure that he'll say, "Libier, I'm done with you. I'm outta here." But I am working toward changing that belief system that I have to do to be loved. God just loves you and me. Nothing can separate us from his love. Especially not our shortcomings. He gave his life so we could have ours. Before we even knew him or loved him, he gave himself up for our hearts. He knows what you need at the right time.

He will always love you, lead you, and keep you. Continue to press forward leaning into God. He will direct your steps.

Please don't misunderstand my Corazoncito. I see nothing wrong with having a life that is thriving and accomplishing things and feeling great. I just think it's all empty if we do it without God or for our own glory. It will never satisfy the soul as we think it will. When you've strived so hard to accomplish something you've wanted your whole life to finally feel whole and worthy, it won't feel good when you get to the destination and you feel as empty as ever. Even more so, because you worked so hard on your own for your accomplishments or accolades, you'll realize they've let you down. Nothing can make us feel anything, we make the choice of how we feel by what we think and believe. And we are responsible for the beliefs we have or keep. If you think you're a success right this minute and begin to truly believe it, you will feel successful. Nothing and no one can make us feel anything. The choice to partner with a belief system and the thoughts that belief provides our brains are within us. If something isn't serving you, you have the power to change. We are responsible for the thoughts we are thinking. What freedom, right?

God will never let you down. If you fill up on him and start to believe that you already are worthy in and through God, you will behave much differently! You have value even when you do nothing of value. Perspectives start to shift, and you live for so much more, without the need of external stimuli to keep you up. Or for an accomplishment, title, dream to finally declare that you have arrived! I honestly don't believe there will ever be a time of "arrival" on earth. I believe the moment someone gives his or her life over to God is the biggest success of his or her life. It won't be easy. Sometimes it might be more difficult than when you were living life for yourself. But you'll find peace no accomplishment on this earth can give you. No money can buy what Jesus paid to give us, and we can, in faith, receive an inheritance beyond our wildest imagination! And in him, we can feel free to accomplish what we were created to do without the need for it to fill the gaping void in our souls.

I read a beautiful book called Captivating by John and Stasi Eldredge, and in the book, they say that men have a question they are trying to answer with everything they set out to do in life. They ask, "Do I have what it takes?" And women have a different question. They ask, "Am I lovely? Do you see me?" I believe this to be true in my own life. In my search for stardom, I was trying so desperately to answer that question for myself. I'm so glad God didn't allow my dreams to precede his love for me. Now I know I am lovely because of what I read in the Bible, it has become a source of great joy for me. It's my love letter from my perfect heavenly Father. It's saved my life and has helped me discover whose I am. I love this psalm. It's so beautiful, and I read it when I feel afraid.

Psalm 23

"The Lord is my shepherd; I shall not be in want [He will never put you in a place where you don't have all you truly need, no matter the pain or suffering, you'll sometimes feel in healing, he will always have you and will never let you go!].

He maketh me to lie down in green pastures: he leadeth me beside the still waters [In times when you're getting ahead of yourself, he'll quiet you with a circumstance so you'll come back to him so you can remember to rest in his love].

He restoreth my soul: he leadeth me in the paths of righteousness for his name's sake [There's nothing he can't heal you from, it might take some time and a big fight from your part, but he will always heal you and lead you in the right direction. You can fail him, but he will never fail you!].

Yea, though I walk through the valley of the shadow of death, I will fear no evil: for thou art with me; thy rod and thy staff they comfort me [And through the valley, you shall walk. It's life and will our highs and lows, in the places he will place you, fear will try to choke out your faith, hope, and joy. But he will comfort you if you turn your mind to him and exalt him over every fear that rises in your heart and mind. Fear is just false evidence appearing real. God is bigger than your fears, and his perfect love will drive out your fear. All of it.].

Thou preparest a table before me in the presence of mine enemies: thou anointest my head with oil; my cup runneth over [He will show his power and glory through your life, people will notice something is different about you, you will have plenty of all you need and more blessings you can count, for the sake of his name being glorified!].

Surely goodness and mercy shall follow me all the days of my life: and I will dwell in the house of the Lord forever [You can count on him loving you every day, being good to you, and giving you his forgiveness as a gift. Even when you blow it royally, he will have the audacity to forgive you if you ask. And you can be sure to spend the rest of eternity with him. That's our hope and light of our life!]."

22

MY WHY

A few weeks before Thanksgiving, on November 25, 2014, I felt as though I was done crying my eyeballs out from healing every day. I kid you not that for that entire year, I had been crying. It was as if all the tears of my life that I bottled up were finally released. But November came, and I went through a few weeks of being super uncomfortable because the tears had run dry. I would try to make myself cry, just because that was my new norm, but nothing would come out. I honestly didn't know what to do after a few weeks of this. I had become so accustomed to my new way of life: reading my Bible and healing through the pain, crying, panic attacks, anxiety, and hopefulness in the midst of chaos, pain, and tears. I knew God said he wouldn't leave me as I was, so I had some faith, but in the deepest parts of me, I was a little afraid I would never come to know a normal life again. I was afraid I would remain depressed and without purpose. When I felt these emotions, I chose to read my Bible and be filled with truth. Changing the way I thought was huge in my healing. I didn't take any medicine through it all. I know medicine is not bad, but for a girl who struggled with addiction, I knew it wasn't the way for me. God's Word was medicine to my soul! He healed me by his Word. I was so depressed and anxious, and he healed me. November came, and the tears ran dry. I was feeling better, so I began to pray for God to help me focus on something else. I wanted to start a new chapter. I prayed God would help me start something that would allow me to leave this painful season behind. I wanted to be done with emotional pain for a while and go help someone else!

God answered my prayers quickly and introduced me to Leah Jonet! Can we say #Queen!? She is pretty much one of the most courageous humans I've had the honor to know personally, as of yet! Leah was the owner and co-founder of, Bridget's Dream, a non- profit organization that helped girls out of human trafficking. I had been following Leah for a while on Facebook. The way she wrote and spoke motivated and inspired me to be the best I could be! She was so passionate about seeing girls know their worth and value. She had been trafficked herself so she understood the pain. She displayed bravery and vulnerability. The way she spoke of God and what she was able to overcome made me feel like I could too! And because of Splashed, I was super moved by anyone in the anti-human trafficking movement, especially in Sacramento. I would sit in my room and read all Leah had to say. I watched TV interviews with her and felt so inspired by her vulnerability and the strength that the Lord bestowed on her. She has gone through some of the most difficult things any baby girl could ever go through, and yet she chose life over death; she chose to die to herself every time she shared her story, to help someone else. That takes so much courage and guts. Putting yourself out there for someone else's sake? It takes bravery, and she did it. She certainly helped me through sharing herself and her story. Even though I had never been trafficked, I had been hurt in similar ways. She gave me hope I would eventually be okay. Her life gave me hope. She was so inspirational and beautiful.

I saw on a Facebook post that it was Giving Tuesday, so I decided to give to Bridget's Dream. I took a bunch of gift cards to donate and got to meet her and speak with her. You know the Lord says that "it is more blessed to give than to receive" (Acts 20:35). I was beginning to experience that. I felt so good that morning after meeting Leah and Stephanie (her executive assistant). As I spoke with them, I felt this enormous call in my gut to make a bigger difference than just Target gift cards. I asked Leah how I could help more and pray for Bridget's Dream. At that time, she said they were looking into opening up a 24/7 drop-in facility that would help victims of human trafficking, giving them a place to go and be restored the only way we all knew we had been restored, the gospel. I knew I wanted to help, but I knew the only real way I could help was to use the talent and ability God had given me. I felt that with all the healing I had done and with the wisdom of becoming the artist God had made me, I had to somehow implement my gifts into helping out a cause I was passionate about. I knew it would require so much dying to my pride here; however, I was on fire for God and wanted to help anyone who had been through what I had been through. I didn't care about what would happen to me. I just wanted to be used in a way that made my broken past have a meaning and a purpose. A fire set in my soul so powerful it drove everything I've done from that time to this date. I think I've lived more in these past few years of my life than the other thirty. Fear and all, I chose to move forward, and it has yielded the best results. I found myself by losing myself, and I started on a journey of living my life for God. "Whoever finds their life will lose it, and whoever loses their life for my sake will find it" (Matthew 10:39). And in hindsight, it's been the most beautiful thing to see all of it unfold. God is faithful.

Some of my biggest prayers while crying in my closet where, "Lord, use this broken life somehow. Provide a place for me to share my story so that no little girl or boy who has been hurt like me will ever have to feel ashamed or like damaged goods." I would pray for photo shoots. It sounds weird. But I did. I was beginning to know who Jesus was, and the Bible gave me the confidence to ask. "Whatever I asked in prayer, I would revive if I had faith" (Matthew 21: 21–22). I knew that even if I prayed for something crazy, God could edit my prayers. I was starting to learn about the abundance of my God. I began praying for a vision for my creative life. Vision to use all the wisdom from my own life that God had given me. I prayed that my life would reflect his glorious name. The verse that saved my life that year would come to life: "You intended to harm me, but God intended it for good to accomplish what is now being done, the saving of many lives" (Genesis 50:20). In my journey through the Wilderness, I began to see the light at the end of the tunnel. I would wake up excited about the adventure God had in store. I didn't know how it would all work out, but I knew the God who'd carried my limp body through some of the wildest parts of my journey, and I trusted him

more than I ever had.

23

#TOSELFIEORNOTTOSELFIE

Remember how I prayed for photo shoots? He answered my first prayer request. I was asked to be a part of a panel of judges for the Reina Fiestas Patrias, here in Sacramento. It's an annual beauty pageant held at the Crest Theatre, featuring beautiful Mexican women representing a region of Mexico, which they showcase in their speeches and gowns. It was a great event and the first time I've ever judged anyone in my life, ha! Well at least it was for a good cause, right? I happened to meet Vincent Gotti while at the event, a photographer who worked with my friend Ozzie, the one who did my hair for the premier of Splashed. Vincent in passing said he would love to do a photo shoot with me. I was in a bit of shock because I had secretly been following him on Facebook. His pictures were beautiful! But I didn't know what his intentions were with me, so I questioned his motives, as I questioned everything in life.

Pessimistic of the outcome, I said something like, "Why?" "So you could have pictures." Ha! Nothing was arranged, but weeks went by, and I prayed and prayed about it because I kept replaying the event in my head. After all, I did pray for photo shoots, right? I talked it over with my husband, and he kept telling me, "Libier, you have a voice. If they ask you to do anything you don't want to do, you can just say no." What a concept: I have a voice, and I can say no if I feel uncomfortable! I messaged Vincent and asked if his offer was still available to do a photo shoot with me. He said yes, and I got super excited until I wasn't and felt confronted by fear. The night before the shoot, I almost called and canceled on Vincent. I was afraid. I hadn't done anything like that in a long time. Put myself out there. Yes, I had done the movie, and now I had a sneaking suspicion that God created me with the talents and abilities and physical nature he did, for a very special and unique reason. I just hadn't experienced those feelings of severe fear in pursuit of creating art. Instead of canceling, I asked my husband to pray for me, and as his words left his mouth, the feelings of fear dissipated. It's amazing what prayer can do. What an amazing blessing has Doug been to me. A man who will pray over me continuously. I cry thinking about the gift God has given me in my husband. We are certainly not a perfect couple however, I am so grateful for him in my life. It's made all the difference in our marriage being able to pray together and for each other.

As I arrived at the shoot location, I sat in Ozzie's chair to get all dolled up for the photos. He was going to do my hair and makeup this time.

I was so excited; I was shimmying and singing. As I sat in the chair receiving rolls in my hair, the gorgeous winner of the event I judged, The Reina Fiestas Patrias, was shooting before me. She was gorgeous, tall, and slender. Every piece of clothing they placed on her amazing frame looked so beautiful. In times past, this would have destroyed my confidence because I was petite and full of curves. I would always compare myself to those of a taller stature. I didn't feel enough in my own skin. Through my year in the Wilderness, I learned that I have no one to compete with. That it feels better to encourage people in their beauty, rather than feel jealous or envious! So here I had an opportunity to act differently so I did. My heart was grateful!

I had no makeup on, my hair looked as if I were in a movie for aliens, and I sat there being okay being me in my transitional state from natural to glam. I allowed her to be her in all her glory. My heart wasn't trying to compete. What a miracle! I didn't feel one ounce of jealousy toward her. I was delighting in her beauty! It's one thing to think you've changed in a certain area of your life but another to see that change in action. I used to be so insecure that whenever I was in a room with a woman who I thought was "more attractive, skinnier, or fill in the blank" than me, I would crawl into my mind and allow the thoughts of all I lacked to consume me. I would have the saddest, most unkind verbiage in my head about myself. But on that day, I loved every part of me. It didn't matter that Cruz was two of me in tallness and gorgeous as gorgeous can be. As I sat smelling my bleached hair being curled, I thanked God for being able to appreciate her beauty. Because I was so sure of mine, I didn't have to succumb to jealous thoughts about her, and I could enjoy her beauty as God intended it. He made her so I could delight in her and see a glimpse of his beauty! It was a gorgeous experience. I knew the way she was made was not the way God intended me to be, and her beauty did not take from mine. We were just different—not one better than the other—just different. Uniquely made by an amazing God. In the present time, one of my very favorite things to do is to encourage women to know their beauty. I feel myself becoming more beautiful when a sister of mine sees herself as her daddy in heaven made her! It's a passion of mine to give out compliments as if they're going out of style. I used to think them. Now I say them. Everyone is in need of encouragement. A few seconds of your time to compliment someone for something you see in that person might be all he or she needs that day to have the confidence to do something important, and the interesting thing is that the love you give out ministers to you. You get to feel that love. It's for you too! Love feels so much better than envy. Envy says we cannot coexist because there is not enough (blank) to go around. Love says God is abundant, and there is a place for both of us here, and more!

The photo shoot was so much fun! I was so happy I didn't cancel because of the uncomfortable wave of emotion I felt from fear of the unknown! When Vincent sent me the pictures I thought, Wowaweewa! These photos are gorgeous. Can we just be really happy for me here? I have never in my life before this past couple of years truly believed in my beauty. I was created in the image of God, and he made me beautiful for his sake. I praise him for I am no longer stuck in pride toggling from feelings of superiority to feelings of unworthiness. I feel secure in my identity because it's in God, and nothing can take value from me. Praise Jesus, Hallelujah! Purposefully made for a purpose only I can attain, not in competition with anyone, free to be all of me. When I saw these photos, I felt this overwhelming courage to use everything God had given me for his glory, beginning with my image. I got the idea that I should use these photos to ask companies if they'd let me model for them, and instead of paying me, they could donate to Bridget's Dream. I can remember always wanting to be a model. If you ask me, I invented the selfie with the film camera! Just ask my mom. Here I was, a thirty-year-old woman, finally allowing my beauty to be a part of my purpose. I believed in my beauty because by accepting it, I acknowledged to myself that I was made in the image of a beautiful creator. What did I gain in years past pretending to be humble trying to convince myself and others I didn't really think I was beautiful? What did self-hatred give me? A plethora of issues. I was beginning to see myself as God saw me. Beautiful. I saw these pictures, and I thought, I can use what beauty the good Lord gave me to raise money for Bridget's Dream.

And so my journey began.

I started emailing every big company I dreamed of working with, including Tiffany & Co, Louis Vuitton, Neiman Marcus, Lexus, and Nordstrom. I even sent one via mail to Steven Spielberg. The God who gave me life again gave me hope that with him, all things were possible! I believed that the God who saved me from myself in the year through the Wilderness was big enough to open doors no man could shut. And if it was in his will, I would be given an opportunity to use the talent and ability he'd placed within me to raise money for the drop-in facility at Bridget's Dream. The following is the letter I sent along with my photos!

To whom it may concern:

My name is Libier Reynolds. I am an actor, dancer, singer, and model from Sacramento, CA. I recently starred in the independent IMDb-accredited film, Splashed. This movie has to do with human trafficking, and it has changed my life knowing the devastation going on in our country, let alone in my own city. The capital of California is one of many American cities identified by the FBI as a hub for sex trafficking.

I am suggesting something radical in order to raise half-a-million dollars for an organization here in Sacramento called Bridget's Dream. They help children and women who have been abused in the human-trafficking world. They would love to build an on-site facility that would house services designed to empower and restore these souls who have been badly wounded. I would like to offer myself in the capacity of an actor or model to raise the funds necessary for this organization. I am suggesting that you would consider having me as your model or actor for a cause. It would be only for a short season.

My hope and prayer is that many hearts would be moved to use me and that the funds would be raised in a miraculous manner. I have faith that this is possible with the help of giving hearts. I would love to speak to someone further about this to share my ideas about it. Thank you so much for your time in reading and considering my letter. I write to you with an extremely heavy heart for all these hurting people who need help. The help is willing, but the funds are lacking. However, I also write this letter with a joyful excitement to see what will come from this.

From a business standpoint, this is a really cool idea for your company to help a cause in a creative way by using someone who is willing to give 100 percent of her pay to an organization that will provide hope and a future for hearts that have been previously devastated. Imagine that you could be a piece of the puzzle in a plan so divine that it would restore and redeem who knows how many souls. I am not naive to the fact that I probably can't stop human trafficking. It is a vicious, devastating, and worldwide issue that is perpetuated by demand. I do, however, have the hope that in the midst of all of this darkness and despair, a light will shine that is brighter, and it will shine more in the darkness. I want to hope and believe there are people in this world who want to make a difference. I thank you once again for your time.

Libier Reynolds

After I wrote this, I truly felt God would do miracles. I was sure the outcome would be good.

Oh, my beloved friend, did he do miracles? He did so in a way I could have never imagined. I was so filled with faith in this time of my life, and I had all this passion to help someone who couldn't perhaps help himself or herself, and that purpose drove me to discover things about myself I never thought I would discover. Faith and meaning are the fires that propelled me forward each day as I faced what I like to call Rejection City! I called so many companies. I wrote so many emails. I made it my full-time job to contact anyone who'd listen to me. I got on the phone and had so much confidence that I could talk to anyone. I got connected with the vice president of communication for Neiman Marcus and pitched the idea to her. She declined the offer.

But I called her anyway. I finally had a voice and I wanted to use it for those who still didn't! God gave me so much courage.

I was determined to help my community, and my pride didn't hinder me. It wasn't for me, so I pressed forward each day, rejection after rejection, I pressed on. I had been so faithless for so many years of my life. It felt great to be filled with this much faith. I felt like a little kid again. The pain of rejection stung like a teenage breakup, but I persisted because I knew it wasn't personal. I was willing to go through the pain because I had a purpose. I didn't care how far I had to go in order to help those from my community who believed they weren't wanted or loved. I have two little girls myself, and it broke my heart that there was such evil in this world. I cried when I got no's, and I screamed like a crazy person anytime I saw the hope of something and it didn't happen. There were so many people who were moved by the attempt. I was on cloud nine. Finally, after so long of being dead to my dreams, I had been resurrected, and I felt great! But there was a sense that I was all alone. I knew God for sure was with me; I couldn't have woken up each day to do it over again if it wasn't for his supernatural strength within me, but I felt as though no one understood my cause. Or no one really cared about it or about me. I started doing it because I thought God would do something right away. I was willing to fight for these girls and boys who were being trafficked, but I still didn't have much love for myself. I was starting to, but my journey began in self-hatred. We were in the middle of it all. Even though the Wilderness was less prevalent, we were still there. God still had a lot of healing in store for me. After so many months of rejection and no success in my perception, I began feeling lonely and misunderstood. My courage and faith started to waver a bit.

24

NO!

Still no yeses. Still no funds for Bridget's Dream.

Two months of nothing working out the way I thought. I wasn't raising any money. I wasn't booking any jobs with any of the talents I finally started to believe in! I began seeking God and questioning if I had heard him right! You ever have those moments? Of like was this me or was that God? Yeah, I started questioning, doubting because it didn't fit my timeline. I wanted microwave results in a crockpot recipe. So I did the best thing I do, I prayed I surrendered my timeline and my result-expectation and sought to be at the heart of God again to find clarity on what I should do at that very moment. I kid you not, I felt God saying to write a song. Me? How? I am not musical. I don't play an instrument and I've never even imagined being a songwriter. I still had trouble singing in front of others. Was this from God or me? At that moment I believe that it was from God because me writing a song would have to have his supernatural intervention, ha! In my eyes, it became apparent that writing a song to raise the money would be the answer! If I had a song, people would so easily download it since it was quick and easy and only ninety-nine cents! Why wouldn't people want to download a song that was going to help kids out of human trafficking? When God asked me to write this song, I legitimately thought he was going to do a miracle and bring five-hundred thousand dollars for Bridget's Dream through my song. I had no doubt God could do it, so I obeyed him. I wrote my song, New! This was probably one of the wildest, most audacious things the Lord has ever whispered into my spirit. I had never in a billion years considered I would write a song. Let alone sing it for anyone. I was terrified of singing in front of people. I don't think you understand the panic I felt each time I had to do a singing audition anywhere. I would freeze. I would feel my throat closing up, and my hands drenched in sweat.

In my mind, there was no way I could write a song. I hadn't even had any music training, and I didn't know how to play any instrument. So why would I be qualified to write a song? Well, this is where the miraculous comes in. God doesn't call us to qualify ourselves through our natural gifting. He calls us to be his servants so we would experience him through our calling and bless others and serve others that they might delight in him. He calls us so we would humble ourselves before him, and truly depend deeply on him. We have a hard time doing that when we are operating out of pride and in the places where we feel vastly sufficient. He wants us to know that his grace is enough for us. He longs for his love, grace, miraculous power in us to be present and awakened. Jesus Christ died so we could live and have life abundant. What does that look like to you? To me, living abundantly included utilizing my creativity for the good works the Lord prepared beforehand for me. How could he do that without me getting proud of what I could accomplish on my natural strength? He picked something I wasn't good at and terrified of, so he could get the glory. Especially from me! It's so easy to stay in the box of what we know how to do. It's not so easy to step out and do what God is calling us to do when we don't feel well equipped for it. We fear the laughter of people who might not understand. But there is much to gain from stepping out in faith. God doesn't let go. You learn something about him and about yourself in the process. When I wrote my song, he said to me, "Sing because I have given you your life back. Sing for joy and shout my praises among all people, no matter what it sounds like. I want you to press on and believe I can do miracles. Despite who will approve or who will like your art, press on. You shall do so through my spirit, so if you boast, you will boast about me."

I wrote the song in a very short time. It was a gift that God would turn all of my sufferings into a beautiful melody. My prayer and hope were that anyone harmed by sexual abuse could cling to my words in this song about how everything was going to be made new. I was on fire for God. He helped me accomplish the impossible through his all-surpassing power, and through the help of Ryan Farrington, I had a recording with my song. Thank you, God, and thank you, Ryan. You rock! I held it dear to my heart. When I put it out on iTunes, I felt pain like never before. I felt like my insides were just out there for anyone to see. I felt so vulnerable. But I also felt more courage when I imagined anyone believing in God or being encouraged by my song and story.

After recording the song, I ended up singing it on a special news story on Spanish Television! What!? Talk about being put way outside of your comfort zone. Karina Banda, a reporter from Univision, interviewed me about my childhood and the abuse I overcame, and then at the end, they played the song. A couple of weeks later, they had me back on the air singing it on live television! What in the world? How do you go from being terrified to sing- to writing a song and singing it twice on television? God, that's how! I was so happy to see the progress. Could I have performed it better? Yes. Could the recording of the song sound better? Yes. But I believe God is more interested in what he's teaching us in the process than in creating a "perfect" product. Perfection is an illusion. I remember the morning of my live singing segment. I was extremely nervous. You know the inner critic loves to attack right before a performance or any big event. I claimed God's peace over myself and knelt before him in the bathroom of Univision. With the courage that the Lord gave me, I went to get my microphone and pressed forward. When I watched it back, I could tell I was extremely nervous. But I sang anyway!I sang for all those whose voice is still trapped in the wounds of abuse. I sang so that anyone hurting would hear me and have hope that they too would one day have their joy back! My heart wanted to come out of my throat, but my voice didn't seize. I couldn't help but think, this was the start of something new, and I can only get better from here if I practice. This was in June of 2015.

In February of 2015, I was trying to figure out how to get people to come onto my website so they could buy the song that would help Bridget's Dream! I felt brand-new and ready for this season of my life. I knew I needed something to do daily to get traffic onto my website. I was asking people to donate for Bridget's Dream there, so I got the idea of doing outfit posts with #ootd (Outfits Of The Day)! I would take a photo each day of what I was wearing and blog about it. I hoped this would create traffic and people would see there was a much bigger cause to think about once they were on Libier. com. So I went to work. Harder than I've ever worked. People were looking at me like I was crazy, so I perceived. Close friends and family were confused about what I was doing and some said discouraging words to my new Internet activity. I was attacked on every level possible in my pursuit. I had to fight for my dream and vision as I'd never fought before. I just didn't know I was fighting with myself. I didn't truly believe I was enough. I didn't truly believe in myself. I don't know if I fully do now, but the needle has moved more in the direction of self-love and belief. At that time, my standing ground was prayer and the Bible. They helped me stay strong when I couldn't go on anymore. There are certain things that will tear you apart if you're not armed with God's armor each day. For months, I fought like a soldier in prayer. I read my Bible, stayed close to God. I knew I couldn't do what he was asking me to do otherwise. But I felt so alone. No one got my vision. And no one was behind me, or so I thought. I think in hindsight, it was the devil trying to pin me against my community. And it worked. For a full six months, I felt as if I was going at it all alone. I couldn't understand why nobody cared about human trafficking and why no one donated to end it. I scrolled through Facebook to gather accurate dates and info, and what it looked like to me now was that people did want to help, people did help. I was feeling so alone because I was still healing from so much trauma. I felt alone because I wasn't really doing what I was doing from a place of abundance, and I didn't believe I was worthy of the call in my life. I was trying to prove to myself that my dreams mattered. But at that time I didn't feel good enough to see them through. I was so scared, and in that mess God, still shone brighter than ever. See, God has a plan for all of us, and we can go about it two ways. From our own resources, and then the shebang gets super tough and we dry up because we are drawing from an empty well, and we serve our cause or mission out of scarcity. Or we can go about it from a place of abundance, truly surrendered to the will of God and only seeking to please him and him alone. Dying to the flesh daily and choosing to remain in God's love through adversity. Knowing and believing full well that we are already valuable, worthy in him, and without need to prove ourselves to ourselves or anyone else. Then we can serve from abundance, and that is connected to his living vine of endless supply and support. I was serving out of my scarcity, and yet God still remained faithful, and people still felt his love and grace through my life. Come on, people. Aren't we glad our God is so boss that even when we are a train wreck he can still shine and work through us? I am! I am!

I collaborated with so many amazing people in my pursuit of raising the money. I got so outside of my little box. I stopped believing everyone was out to get me, and I stopped being paranoid and started believing—to quote an amazing book, The Alchemist—"the whole universe is going to help me fulfill my destiny." Looking back at my journey, I have had the opportunity to do so many cool things because of this pursuit, and nothing compares to the relationships and lives I've been able to surround myself with. Dreamers and fighters for a better world! People of no faith who have seen a glimpse of God through my brokenness and people of great faith encouraging me in times of weakness and faithlessness on my behalf. It's been the people and relationships I've made that are a part of my treasure and rich life I get to live in this season!

I've made countless mistakes and had so many "failures." But through it all, God has remained and will remain faithful to complete the good work he began in me (Philippians 1:6). Even though try as I might, I definitely did not raise much money, I earned something that cannot be wasted, stolen, or coveted; I earned seeing myself. Knowledge of who I am. The belief that God did love me and that I have a purpose. Raising money was my focus. Little did I know God was working on a way deeper level, helping me to become what I needed for the next season of my life.

I believe without a shadow of a doubt now that God could have easily given us that half a million. But it wasn't the money that would have changed the hearts of the people on this journey. He knows what we need, and most of the time, it's not gold or silver. At the end of May, I received a phone call from Leah, the founder of Bridget's Dream, saying they were going to be seizing all efforts of fundraising. They came to a place of halt, needing to take a step back as a nonprofit to reevaluate where they would be going next. She was so kind and thanked me for all the work I had put in. I felt as if my world was crashing down. I mean, I had worked my patootie off to make this a reality, and in a five-minute conversation, it was over. The whole reason my blog was in place was for this. The whole reason I wrote a song was for this. The whole reason I fought for my life was for this. Right?

25

ENCOURAGEMENT IS AWESOME

God can take the unlikely - the broken—the uneducated—and he can do wonders through a willing vessel. Any vessel that is willing and believing in him. I believe I am that. Anything you see that is admirable in me, I owe it all to the Lord. God isn't interested in providing what we don't need. He does, however, know what we need before we say a word. And at this time in my life what he knew I needed was an encouraging word and a listening ear. A sweet word can turn someone's discouragement into fuel to keep on going. What impact can you make in the world today by speaking life into somebody's life?! I know and understand the power of a kind word spoken over a very broken spirit and a great pair of listening ears. God gave me my friend, Teresa for this season of my life. She showed me a love in a friendship that was rare. I shared my story with Teresa after not being able to share it with anyone else for many years. She was an amazing listener and she just held space for my pain that I had never experienced. She cried with me and allowed me to spend time grieving what I had for so long held back. She knew nothing she could say would heal me but somehow her listening ears were a better way of helping me than telling me what I should do with my hurt. To this day my friend is one of the most beautiful listeners and I hope to be similar to her for someone else that needs that same friendship that she provides me with! Thank you, Teresa for everything you are to me.

At the beginning of my quest to blogger town, I met Rachael. Rachael was a wonderful person in my life who believed in my God-given dreams the way no one else did. She started babysitting my girls right when I went on this wild adventure of starting my blog. She would talk to me for hours and listen to my crazy vision for raising money for Bridget's Dream. From the beginning, she was so encouraging to me. I tell you what. God sent her into my life to be his mouthpiece. The Lord encouraged me so much through this seventeen-year-old, beautiful soul. She would send me texts out of "nowhere" exactly when I needed them. She would answer some of the prayers through what she said to me. God's placement of Rachael in my life was an important element for me starting to believe in myself and in my ministry! God provided me with encouragement I needed through her. Let's learn from her example and extend an encouraging word to someone in our lives! I had to dig deep to find the encouragement I needed solely through God, and he showed me he was enough, but when my strength was failing me, Rachael came in and, on certain occasions when I wanted to call it quits with my blog, she encouraged me to continue moving forward. I knew it was the Lord through her, but I appreciated her obedience. To this day, she is one of my very closest friends, and I love her to life. Thank you, Rachael!

The word "encouragement" means The action of giving someone support, confidence, or hope.

Growing up, I didn't feel encouraged. I don't know what it was, but I think it's hard to encourage anyone else unless you feel encouraged yourself. I didn't get it from the sources I was craving it from, like my mother or father. I know they did the best with what they had but I don't think either of them was encouraged as children either! The lack of encouragement was the thorn in my side. I "didn't" have it my whole life and so it was difficult to believe in myself. "If they didn't believe in me, why should I?" The lesson I was learning was that the encouragement I was seeking was the Lord's alone. No human is capable of giving that to someone at all times and with the same intensity. I was learning to not seek people, rather accept and receive the approval and love of God which is everlasting, unconditional and already mine. People can disappoint me, and I can disappoint people. If I was tying my success of moving forward as an artist based on the encouragement of others, it would eventually run dry. God is the only source that never runs dry. See for so long I was mad at the people around me who saw all I was doing, yet had nothing good to say! The naysayers, the haters, the pessimistic ones! Or "The Turkey's" as my favorite teacher, Mr. Eick used to say, "Libier, don't let The Turkeys get you down!" But I was. I was focusing on what people weren't validating in me and I began to learn that I could do that for myself.

Little did I know God was positioning me into a great lesson learned. If I don't find myself to be the most encouraging one for myself, no one else's will ever be enough. If I don't go to God for it, no one's will ever be enough. I had the right tools to move forward. God and the knowledge of myself being my own cheerleader. Go, Libier! I believe in you!

The disadvantage of not being properly encouraged my whole life now became a wonderful opportunity to look to God and myself for the encouragement that would not let me down. God's encouragement is available, 24/7. The one who will fill me with it so I can give it out. And that I did. When I began asking God to encourage me in the way I most needed it, he began to fill me with enough to go around to anyone I believed needed it. I became an encouraging machine! I used to never encourage anyone. I didn't know how. I was so afraid of people; I didn't really like to be around people, to be honest. I wasn't interested in anyone's stories. All I could think of when I met someone was, What can they do for me? I had such a hard time relationally and in social aspects. Social anxiety at its finest! I had no desire to know anyone else unless I was really into that person for some reason. I didn't understand how to ask people questions about his or her life. If you had a conversation with me before the Wilderness, I am so sorry. Please forgive me. I didn't know what I was missing. I just didn't know how to encourage or talk to anyone because I had a low self-esteem, and I wasn't encouraged myself. I thought if I gave someone a compliment, he or she would just be puffed up with pride, so I withheld any good thoughts I had about most people. I heard a sermon that changed my life in this regard. Pastor Louis from Warehouse Ministries, bless his heart. He preached on encouragement and the fact that everyone was in need of it. There is not one person who didn't secretly crave it and need it. I have loved the years God has allowed me to encourage anyone. I love to encourage people. I love hearing their stories, and God has given me a passion for helping people realize their God-given dreams and to encourage them in that pursuit. I love this way of being; it feels amazing. I have seen in action how Jesus suggests that it is better to give than it is to receive (Acts 20:35). I am not saying I am all that and a bag of chips and that I don't stumble in this area still! If I'm having a rough day, I'm not a very good listener or encourager! But you better believe I've learned to ask for prayer rather than trying to muster up some false encouragement toward anyone else. Progress, not perfection. I'll be a work in progress until I die. I just love seeing the vast difference in my heart toward being around people and the value I now find in hearing people's stories! We all have one, and we all can learn so much from one another.

26

ARE WE STRIVING?

After months and months of hard work, I started feeling burned out. I was doing things that weren't good for my health or for my family. I started struggling with eating my emotions, again—something I had "under control" for a while. I had not been that stressed out in a long time. I felt the pressure of eradicating human trafficking on my own. I hate that the enemy twisted what began as such good intentions into something toxic for my family and me. I wanted so badly for my pain of being abused to be erased and I had the idea that when I raised money for human trafficking I would somehow feel better. It was my way of making justice, I guess. I quickly found out as Leah called Bridget's Dream off that I had an opportunity to reevaluate why I was doing what I was doing. What started off as a ministry and a cause became an obsession that caused me to behave rudely to my family, and I was running myself ragged, all for personal justice? There was a huge imbalance in my life. I was focused so much on helping others that (1) I wasn't taking care of myself, (2) I wasn't respecting my husband and (3), I wasn't present in the lives of my children. I was always thinking about my mission. It was not balanced, and it was almost neurotic. I knew God said he was just and would turn my pain into joy, but I wanted to take the matter into my own hands in times of great emotional pain. I wanted to have a ministry, but I was serving out of scarcity and my pain, and you know what? Even if we had raised the half-a-million, I wouldn't have felt like I did enough.

If I raise enough money for human trafficking, my heart won't hurt as much from being molested, raped, threatened, abused, and rejected." When I looked deep within that's what I discovered my heart thinking. But even if the money was there, I think I would still have the pain and a slew of new problems and disappointments to work through. Even so, God is sovereign, and he always has the highest and best for us. Sometimes we don't understand what he is doing, but we stumble along but he will remain faithful no matter how many times we need correction and love. God knows the very heart of his people. Sometimes we start certain things because we are passionate about justice. I think we all, deep down, are most passionate about seeing justice in our own hearts and lives and the lives of others. We might start doing things because we think that's what God wants us to do, but I believe God wants our hearts first and foremost. We don't need to be heroes or justifier for he alone can do that. When our "calling" or mission exults our relationship with him it's not in the right order and we began doing things in our own strength to appease our own ego and massage the pain we so desperately want to not feel. God wants to love us to abundance, and from that abundance, we can serve much differently, knowing we are enough without a specific outcome having to come to pass. When he is our focus and our first and then whatever else he's called us to, like our family. Then we can have a mission that is in line with God's purpose for our lives because our mission is in obedience to the Lord, we leave outcomes, timeliness, victories, and justice up to him! The enemy is a fierce opponent, but "greater is he, who is in us than he who is in the world" (1 John 4:4).

With the end of that chapter in my life, I was venturing out to a new adventure. I was asking God for a new direction. We had come this far, now what? I was a little confused but reflecting on all I had gained and learned from this "failed" attempt at raising money for Bridget's Dream with my talent and ability. I had never been in this place before. I had never felt so passionate for a cause in my entire life. I literally was willing to do anything it took to help it. Somedays I felt the weight of the world on my shoulders, and all I could think about were little girls being sold. Then other days I would be so grateful I wasn't in that deep, dark healing place anymore that God had legitimately saved me from myself and all of the PTSD and anxiety. I was so grateful I had a dry eye on most days. I went so strongly into the other direction of not having a purpose and life outside my home. I did my family a little disservice. So much started to come apart. My duties at home were not being done. My husband and children didn't have clean underwear because I was too wrapped up in what I was doing. I didn't see it then, the huge unbalance in my life. All I knew was this vision and fire God had placed deep within me to make a difference in this world. I finally felt important. However, some-times we forget that the biggest difference we will make is in the ordinary lives God has gifted us right here, right now. In the closest relationships he has given us: our spouses, children, families, or close friends he blesses us with. I was all into my calling, and to be honest with you, it felt so good to feel needed in a different way. I didn't feel as if the need in my home that called me to be a janitor or a chef was "good" enough to validate these vast feelings of unworthiness. I thought if I helped human trafficking, I'd finally feel worthy and valuable. I learned that I had to choose those feelings for myself espe-cially as a stay at home mom. I am making a difference in someone's life! My husband and children might never "really" know what I do around the house but God sees me, erry day- aaall day. He notices with which care I make them meals. He sees my crack countless times as I bend over to pick up another toy from the ground. He sees me encourage my husband as he leaves work! He sees me cleaning a dirty toilet bowl with gratitude that I have three to clean that flush properly. He sees my comfort to my little girls when they get hurt. He sees how much I love to keep things organized so people can find their things in our house. He sees it all and it matters because it matters. I matter not matter my title Tis' all!

If Jesus is your plumb line, you don't go too far out of balance in any one area. But because I ran too fast, too soon, I didn't allow the grace of God to cover me, and I hurt my girls and my husband by not being present. I be-gan a fancy juggling act leading myself, and in the midst, I dropped all the im-portant balls. My relationship with my love. Time seeing my little ones grow up. It was as if my new passion for helping a "cause" was now driving me farther away from my first and most important call, to be a wife and a mother. I knew I didn't hear God wrong in that he wanted me to have a vision and a purpose for my life. I heard him clearly when he said I had talent to give. I heard him well when he told me I was meant to be myself and become free from shame and fear. Things got messy when I moved forward and pretended to know where I was going and often forgot about submitting my plans to God. He was waiting for me to come back to him and ask for direction. I saw the rebellion in my heart when my husband asked me a simple question one night. Doug, bless your heart for speaking the truth in love to me.

"Libier, do you feel like you have to prove yourself?" Asked my husband.

I, of course, reacted like a total lady:

"I have nothing to prove!" I yelled so loudly at him knowing the minute the sentence came out of my mouth there was an actual question mark that followed in my soul. That silence and pause gave me the chills.

What was I doing? I felt like I was following God's call on my life, that it wasn't about me, I was serving the Lord. Right? I was saving people from Human Trafficking, right? I was doing something so important that I needed to not be cleaning and cooking, right? That's so beneath me, right?

As the weeks went by, Doug's question engulfed my mind.

"Libier, what are you trying to prove?" His eerie voice in my mind said to me again. Only he's not eerie he's amazing I'm just saying you know when someone truth-bombs you and you can't help but hear it over and over in your Cabeza?

Another truthful sting.

What was I trying to prove? I had been in a cage of fear for so long that when I tasted freedom, all heaven broke loose! All of the sudden, I felt free to be me. I made so many mistakes through it, but I also learned a whole lot. God is so faithful—even in my mess—he still gets the victory. I was trying to prove something, I just didn't know it at the time. I didn't know yet how to just receive the gospel and the gifts God provides freely without having to earn them. My faith was being strengthened. I wanted to make a difference; I knew that. I wanted to discover who I was in Christ. I wanted to see what I was made of. I wanted to prove wrong anyone in my life who doubted me, who made me feel like an idiot for not having a college degree. I wanted people to see that I was more than an attractive frame; I was more than a sexual being. I had value to bring to the table, more than what I did for my household. I had a brain that could think in a beautiful way, not just in a book smart way. I didn't have a diploma to prove my worth or wasn't able to solve a math problem fast enough but I wasn't made to do that. I wanted to be okay with that. I wanted to discover my kind of intelligence. I knew it was in there, somewhere. I wanted to prove that my faith was going to overcome all of my mental illness and not hinder my bright future. I wanted to prove that an immigrant, a woman immigrant who had nothing to her name as far as wealth or riches, could be worth something. I wanted to prove that I could bring in a paycheck with my art. I wanted to prove that the vision God had given me was real and that I wasn't crazy. I wanted to prove that Jesus was in the business of taking the most broken and fragile things and using them for his glory. I wanted to prove that I was worth love and attention. I would be delighted in. I wanted to prove I had something to offer this world.

156

Reading this back in this second draft is completely therapeutic. You should really write out a raging vent like that; you'll discover what's really in your heart. Whoa, Libier; that felt good. Whoa, now I understand a lot of my issues. The problem with trying to prove to other people something about yourself is this. You have no control over how others think or feel about you. And a lot of these feelings can come from assumptions I made, not the truth. The only one you can truly convince that you are worthy is yourself. That's all I needed? To be okay with being enough for me? Holy cow. All of that striving to come to the realization that it was never about others believing in me rather than me believing in myself. Can we go back a couple years so I could save myself some work? Ha! This is beautiful, people. If you are reading this, and you're on a journey to self-love and acceptance, take heart it isn't an easy road. But the freedom you so crave is right here. Right now. Do you want it? That would be a better question. Not, can you have it?

Before I learned this concept and my focus had been on proving myself to others, I started striving. Striving every day to prove this to myself and anyone who would care to see. Exhausting myself in the pursuit of proving all of the above and then some. We can go from one mess to another when we don't die to our flesh and it's desires each day and ask God to fill us up and lead our way, every day!

I went from not believing in myself to believing that God made me look the way I looked for a very specific reason, and I took that and ran with it. I didn't care what people thought about me. I took as many selfies as I could and had no shame in posting my photos on Instagram. I knew I wasn't being "vain." I truly believed God could use me both physically and spiritually to inspire someone. I had the hope that people would look at my photos and see Christ. I had the hope that even as broken as I am/was, people would find hope that they too could be free just as I was beginning to feel. But I strived hard. Even though I found areas of freedom, even though I cared less about what people "thought" about me as I was learning to fear God more, I wanted to be seen as who I was meant to be, how I felt inside. Corrie ten Boom once said, "Always live according to my vision and not my eyes." And I guess I was living that way. But when you live that way, people don't see your vision because it's not theirs to see and their questions or criticism of your vision can come across as discouragement! I had to learn to focus my eyes on God. But some days, pride and ego started being a problem for me, again. It seems as if pride is just one of those things you have to surrender and deal with every day with God. I did have something to prove, so my attitude started displaying that. God didn't call me to prove myself. He called me to be his servant and to know him. I realized I had started my blog, vision, and business with the right intentions, yet somewhere down the road, I strayed from the path of God's will. So I took a much-needed break. I wanted to realign myself with God. I wanted to go back to why I started, and in that time of rest and submission, God showed me that I was enough no matter what I was doing or accomplishing. He allowed me to come to the end of myself and see that it wasn't through works that I was going to gain his love or approval. The Bible says, "For it is by grace you have been saved, through faith—and this is not from yourselves, it is the gift of God—not by works, so that no one can boast" (Ephesians 2: 8–9). For a person like me, "doing" equaled "love". I couldn't understand receiving love without merit. When I became a stay-at-home mom, I went through the deepest depression of my life. It was as if every insecurity was coming out to get me. My whole life, I believed I had to "work" to feel worth. As a stay-at-home mom, I had never been in a place where I wasn't considered part of the workforce, yet I was working more than I had ever worked before without seeing a paycheck. No awards or people seeing my triumphs at a corporate office! At my job, before I stayed home, we had these bells we got to ring each time one of us did a great job. I worked in marketing and bought TV time for infomercials. It was a dynamic place with an amazing culture. It was like working with all your best friends in an open floor plan. No one had a cubicle. I don't know what Bruce and Lisa did to hire such amazing people (high five, guys!), but I met some amazing humans working there. We all had a great work ethic and worked really hard. We also celebrated hard. I went from that environment to being at home, by myself, with my adorable lump of meat. She was amazing. My baby girl was such a huge blessing. I was just broken in so many areas that had to do with my personal worth and how I perceived myself as valuable. So, I started questioning who I was. My deepest fear was that I had tapped out all the dreams in my personal life—that I, Libier the dreamer, would be lost at sea never to return again. I believed it was over for me. That all I was ever going to be was someone's wife and someone's mom. Please hear my heart: I love being a wife and mother, but I love being Libier the dreamer, as a wife and mother, she is much saner! But these are my insecurities talking here at that time of my life. No one rang bells for me when I changed my, one-hundredth diaper. No one praised me for how much I made Maddy giggle. I felt unseen. I had romanticized having a child in so many ways, and in so many ways that expectation slapped me right in the face. I wanted my child to make me whole and happy. I wanted to transfer all of those feelings of my unaccomplished dreams onto her. I wanted to pretend I was okay, so I did. To the common passerby, I was a put together mom who loved being at home and baking her next batch of cupcakes. I will say, in hindsight, I feel extremely grateful for being able to stay at home with my children. I understand some of you are a single parent or someone who craves to stay home, and you are reading this becoming a little angry at my internal, now external, monologue. However, this wasn't my feeling every day. I did enjoy so many moments I hold dear. I just need you to understand how my heart and mind felt so you can see the miraculous nature of God in changing all of that. I started becoming the "perfect" wife and mom. I strived hardcore to become what people would call a bona fide stay at home mom!

At that time though, it cut me to the core, because of how insecure I already was. It tore me up so badly because I was already questioning that about myself as a stay-at-home mother. Am I of any worth? That slip up caused me to tailspin into an even bigger depression, and I started struggling with an eating disorder again. I would be over the toilet, and I would imagine my daughters walking in the same way and I didn't want that. Somehow, some twisted way, I believed it was okay to treat myself that poorly but I would never want my daughters to go through that! In therapy, I realized I had a lot of issues that revolved me being out of control and wanting to desperately to feel some sense of security. I realized that when I felt unsafe or like I needed a sense of control my coping skills were to go to control what I ate and what I purged. I wanted to be different and have different coping skills with this life's uncertainty. I felt like a failure because my endeavors didn't work out as I had planned them, so I reverted back to bulimia. God showed me he is in control! And he'll never let me go! "And I am sure of this, that he who began a good work in you will bring it to completion at the day of Jesus Christ. (Philippians 1:6)" Even if I didn't see the whole picture, I could choose him over the bulimia to cope with my hurt and disappointment. He showed me I was enough and that I didn't have to feel bad for not having measured up in my own eyes. He gave me the freedom to know I was enough in him, no matter what I did. No matter if I was making money, not making money, had a title, a college degree, or no college degree. I was something significant to him because he died to give me life. I began to really believe I mattered. I began to really believe that it was never about striving; it was about receiving. Receiving the worth that comes from Jesus and his sacrifice. It is so bizarre to receive something you don't deserve. It can feel itchy, uncomfortable—trust me, I've tried to do so many things to pay Jesus back.

I went so many years without struggling with bulimia. From 2012 to 2016. I felt like a terrible failure when I relapsed. I couldn't believe that I had walked so far from that and then I was right back where I had started. So much was causing pressure, hardly anyone bought the song, I didn't succeed in raising money I set out to, I was being a poor wife and mother, my home was a disaster. The new and rising blog. The days I wasn't spending time with God and going to him with all my worry and anxiety were days of darkness. This journey has been difficult, but with each difficulty, I've seen Jesus more clearly. I praise God for every struggle because in the moment of despair he became more real to me. Comforted me the only way God can. When I finally noticed that I was not going down a good path, I decided to give myself a seven-day break from blogging and doing anything that involved social media or "work." It was time to realign with my heavenly Father. It was time to stop striving or proving myself.

At the beginning of 2016, I asked God in prayer to show me if I was worthy. I didn't understand the concept that once you accept Jesus as your Lord and Savior, you become worthy by his sacrifice. I had just heard in church that we were all unworthy of God's love, yet he still chose to give it to us. This was a weird concept my heart needed clarity over. Although I had accepted Jesus years ago, I kept feeling as though I still wasn't worthy of God's love or his gifts. I began to ask him to explain to me how I was worthy and to help me believe it. And so our worthy adventure began. God doesn't mess around when we ask him to reveal more of himself to us. He moves mountains for his people to know him better, he is a relational God and we are meant to seek him with all of our hearts! After my prayer I forgot all about it and months later, my worthy question was answered through Melinda Watts, a worship leader and founder of an amazing organization called Glam Camp for Girls. At that time I still had social media and as I scrolled the Instagram I saw she posted a picture of herself wearing a shirt that said "Worthy". She'd said she'd had some extra shirts, and if anyone had wanted a free one, she should shoot her a message. So I did. Then I forgot I did that too.

Needless to say, the word WORTHY ran through the back of my mind. God pursued my heart with it. And then on the anniversary of my mom's attempted suicide, I asked God if I was worthy of his love. I was a wreck emotionally at that time. As even though it had been over a decade since the attempts, my heart still has wounds left to heal. I underestimated the pain I felt and sometimes didn't want to give myself the permission to grieve and show myself compassion for what I had been through. I knew this time I had to show up for myself, take care of myself; my healing depended on it. As I cried, I prayed to the Lord, and I forgot if it was the same day or the very next day, but a package showed up at my house with a shirt that said WORTHY across the chest. I cried in gratitude for a heavenly Father who knew how to comfort his daughter. I wept at his feet just feeling the beginning of a healing journey to believing my worth rests in him, not in what I do! My striving was getting a makeover. I was being freed to just be me.

On Sunday I decided to take my seven-day break I went up for prayer at the altar of my church. Christine, a friend and prayer volunteer of the church, waited eagerly to know how to pray for me. I looked at her and said, "I am struggling with bulimia." She began praying for me; she told me Jesus wanted to love me and give me gifts, but I needed to stop resisting him. As she prayed in my ear I felt God speaking right to my heart. He made me believe that he saw my pain and the struggle with my eating disorder. He made me believe that I wouldn't remain the same that he was going to help me. Her prayer really gave me so much hope and it helped me to understand the gospel of Jesus even further! Much of my life, I believed I had to give, sometimes even toxically, in order to "please" everyone into not leaving me or loving me. I have never experienced a love that just loves for love's sake. Too much of me had been taken for me to understand right away how God loved me. It was strange to me that he could just love me, for me. And that he delighted in me. Not just tolerated me. This woman who prayed for me didn't know I hadn't been singing for a whole month, not even during worship at our new church because I began to believe I wasn't good enough, again! In her prayer, she said, "God wants you to worship him with his voice, not caring what other people have to say about you." BOOM. God speaks through people when we are ready to listen. I had begun doubting the gifts God had given me, again. I had begun to allow pride and my ego to engulf the ability and talent and joy in singing God had begun to free up in me. I felt freedom in singing, and I truly saw I was getting better at it because I was practicing more. And pride and ego started to take that freedom from me again. But as I listened to her prayer I made it a point to give it back to God. To believe my worth is in God's love, not in the opinion of men. God did not mean for us to stay in the same place. He wants us to go from glory to glory. And get better and better to reflect his glory! After her prayer, I wept and wept. God knew me so well, and he used a prayer warrior to lead me into the next season of my life; Writing and composing my second recorded song, "Worthy." Available on iTunes or Spotify!

Composer? What? In July of 2015, God gave me the gift of playing the piano overnight. Miracle, if you ask me. Here's my blog from that time.

You'll never believe what happened to me this weekend! Last Wednesday was my first piano class. I really want to learn so I can write my own music to all the songs I'm writing. I learned the very basics of the piano. Middle C and all.

I don't know if you know this, but I lead worship at my church for our junior and high school loves. I only sing, and someone else plays the guitar. This weekend, he wasn't going to be able to play with me, so I still wanted to figure out a way to do worship with the group. My husband suggested me trying to learn an easy song on the piano. I thought I would give it a shot. This was Friday night. So I went to my college; YouTube! And found a piano tutorial. The guy explained what to do, and I did it. I don't know how to explain to you that I just played. I saw what he did and then, from memory, just played the entire song with both hands and correct rhythm. Wow! Crazy. I have never experienced something so bizarre, going from never doing something to full-on doing it as if I had been doing it my whole life. Miracle. What? My husband was so delighted; I was so delighted.

It was God working through me. I was able to lead worship with one song and one very crazy story about how God just showed me how to play piano in an hour. I don't know if that affected any of the people in that room. But I'll tell you what. It affected me. I have a newfound love for God and believe he can really do anything for his glory. I could think I was just that talented that I taught myself to play the piano in an hour. But I can't even for a second believe that. Before my Wednesday piano class, I prayed and asked God to help me learn it. I asked God to have it be as if I just remembering how to play, that I would be able to have brain plasticity as a child and soak up all my piano lessons. Well, he did more than that. I am in awe of God. I am in awe of all things right now. I feel shaky even writing this to you. I do believe God planted that gift within me. But I've had to stop being so afraid of failure for him to help me reclaim who I am. This has been the adventure of my life, and I am thrilled at the possibilities of the future, providing God gives me more precious time on this earth. So with that, I leave you. I hope you are encouraged and excited about the fun exciting gifts God has planted in you. When our hearts are surrendered to him, everything is possible. Your dreams with God are possible. I love you.

Stay blessed. Stay saucy.

Libier

I made room for God and he gave me more than a song about being Worthy in his name. No more striving. Every day, surrender to being. I was trying to prove something, but God showed me he paid the ultimate price for my freedom, and I could receive him in faith and gratitude. So each day, I receive all he has for me. It's getting easier and easier to understand I don't have to do anything to keep his love. What freedom!

27

FATHER ISSUES

God is healing me from abandonment and not being able to experience the constant love, encouragement, fellowship, or discipline of my father. I'm healing from very painful wounds caused when my daddy was deep in his addiction giving his life to alcohol instead of his family. I understand so much as a thirty-two-year-old woman. I can see the pain behind my daddy's life. When I turned one, my father endured the most traumatic thing in his life. His brother died tragically in a car accident. I just realized this very recently. I didn't remember. As an adult, you can see things differently, perhaps put yourself in other's shoes. I can't imagine what it would be like to lose one of my brothers like my father lost his. What he felt when walking into a morgue to verify the identity of his brother who endured a horrific accident. The eyes of my daddy's heart were never same. I know at that time my dad didn't believe in Jesus and didn't experience the peace that surpasses all our understanding as one gets when Jesus is in our heart! He couldn't see the hope of God turning this horrible situation into good. I can only imagine that this deep pain drove him into more addiction.

I didn't have him as a dad. But understanding a little more of his pain eases my own.

I now understand it wasn't because of me that he didn't want a relationship with me. His heart was just hurting so much. I don't understand all of the brokenness he suffered that caused him to question his own worth. Possibly wondering if he had what it took to be my father or a husband to my mother. His answer was alcohol because, in my perspective, it probably terrified him that he might not know how to be whom we needed. I'm not saying some of the hurtful things he did were right. I believe that's between God and him. But I am now understanding on a deeper level. One day, my daughters are going to find ways I've hurt them, and my only hope is that they'll choose forgiveness and understanding. For me personally, if Jesus can forgive me in all I've done, I can forgive all of those who've wronged me. Jesus has shown me how to see my dad as he sees him and I have forgiven him. It has not been overnight, that's for sure! The deep wounds that were done over so many years left me marred and questioning my own identity. Questioning whether I was of any importance to anyone. Whether I had anything to give. I would wonder if I had any value, and the answer always felt like a big, fatty no. I didn't feel seen or wanted. I lived out in rebellion to that assumption, trying to prove my way into value and worth. Calling out for attention in any way I could. I was crippled by perfectionism and self-hatred, I hated who I was because I believed I was annoying and a burden. I believed what I had to say wasn't important. No, my daddy never told me words like these, at least, I don't remember that. It was his emotional absence that sent that message loud and clear to my soul. I believed I was an annoyance and that self-proclaimed prophecy played out every day of my life, I so easily found evidence for it. It was what I focused on.

What happens to a little girl who didn't get any attention from her father, causing her to crave healthy touch, love, and attention, who grows up in the scarcity of it for many years, and then hits puberty, and beauty is in her that attracts boys? My beauty hurt me; it betrayed me. I figured out really quickly that to be loved meant I had to do something for it or give something away that felt wrong and uncomfortable. But I did it because I was hurting for healthy touch. I was starving for someone's attention and love. Only through my performance was I ever to feel any praise or love. Competitiveness and jealousy of anyone else that made me feel "threatened." Man, what a sad and lonely way to live. Thank God he had a different way for me. Thank God he saw me and he's never left me and has begun a good work in me that he will bring to completion (Philippians 1:6).

My dad is a new man today. He has been sober for almost eight or nine years now. As I type this, I can recall in the past year so many instances of God redeeming our relationship. He and I took my two little girls to a park the other day, and as he was pushing my toddler on the swings, I sat on the other swing to rest for a quick minute. I sat there and suddenly felt the warmth of his hand pushing my upper back, and off I went. I felt the

169

gorgeous breeze as my father pushed his thirty-two-year-old little girl in a swing, and tears of gratitude rolled down my cheeks for this precious moment. Hoping he wouldn't see me, I sobbed silently and praised God for this redeeming moment. I thank God for that time, it was the Lord himself gifting that moment to me as a reward for my obedience in wanting to forgive this man I called my father.

I could have easily not wanted a relationship with someone who hurt me so much, but I knew God would do something amazing if I gave into fully healing from all the brokenness in my past. I just never expected my dad to be my dad when I was thirty-two years old, and it made my heart leap for joy as if I were a six-year-old. I know that's how it played out for me because God is so intentional, and he gives good gifts that make sense and are specific to our story. I know some of you might not know your father, or he might be gone. Some of you might not want a relationship with yours. If that's what you believe is best for your healing at this time, do what is necessary to heal, and be willing to do what God wants for your life. A year prior, I was so angry with my father, and I couldn't even talk to him without physical pain. So this instance didn't just happen. I grieved him, and a part of grief is anger. Now I don't feel that way towards him or my mother. I feel gratitude for all of my family and all of my past!

I would lovingly suggest that you'd be hopeful and expectant that God will do miracles of redemption in your life, that are very special and specific to your story as you allow him to heal you from whatever has broken your heart. A few years ago, my heart hurt terribly each time my father would be affectionate toward my children. I couldn't understand my feelings.

I was almost mad at myself for feeling that way. I felt jealous of his affection toward them because I never felt it as a kid. Funny how unresolved issues in our hearts will always rear their heads when we are triggered by someone or something. Now that I've healed the same action makes my heart fill with gladness for my girls to have their Abuelito! My dad wasn't sober for my childhood, but God has healed him so he can be for my two little princesses. He loves them so much. He loves them in a way that brought a lot of pain to my heart because I couldn't understand why I didn't receive that love and attention as a young child and even now as a "big kid." But, there's been so much healing in my heart that when he displays his love for them, I cherish every moment. It feels like payback. It's not targeted at me, but I hear every kind word he gives them—his attention and concern—and take it as my own.

As a kid, I developed an attitude toward my father that said, "Oh, you don't want me? I will show you why you should've when I (enter any achievement). I will prove to you that you should've wanted me all along. I was worth the fight, but you missed out, so now I am (whatever achievement). I hope you realize how stupid you were for not wanting me. I'll show you. And I hope it hurts you as much as you hurt me"

I also developed an independence that said, "Well if that's how you'll be, this is how I'll be. I'll guard my heart so much that I won't need anyone, ever. I will never need any person to make me (fill in the blank). I don't need anyone." And so it went that my outward "tough" shell eventually built up my calloused heart, and I indeed felt as if I truly didn't need anyone. I wanted no one. I loved no one. Not even myself. But then I trapped myself in because I felt as if no one needed me, no one wanted me, and no one truly loved me.

I was so relationally jaded; I didn't trust. I didn't love. My relationships were always surface level, and I honestly only cared about what the person could do for me. Could he or she fill the void with his or her time and attention and do only what I want from him or her without my need to reciprocate any effort toward the relationship? If the person didn't, out he or she went from my circle. Emotional pain is crazy. You can't see it, but it's so painful sometimes we try to numb it with other things. Well I know I want to do it soberly, so I endure the pain in God's strength. I want complete breakthrough from my chains. Not a temporary distraction to my issues. The holes that the absence of my father created in my heart are now scars I can remember without pain. I understand my father, my family, and myself more. I love more fiercely now. Love is going out and coming in, and I have never felt better. Love always wins. Love always prevails. But I couldn't have done it without going through the pain of healing.

28

WORDS ARE POWERFUL

I believe there is power in the thoughts and words we say. We so often make friends with our ailments that it becomes who we are. I have claimed with such conviction so many useless things in my life. It seems as though what we say has no importance, but out of the abundance of the heart, the mouth speaks. "A good man brings good things out of the good stored up in his heart, and an evil man brings evil things out of the evil stored up in his heart. For the mouth speaks what the heart is full of" (Luke 6:45).

Things I have claimed over and over in my life with such ease include the following.

I am addicted to food.

I'm a shopaholic.

I can't sing.

I have no self-control.

I am always overweight.

I don't have what it takes.

I have anxiety.

I have depression.

I am not good with money.

I am uneducated.

I am not qualified for the call of God in my life.

I am done partnering with all of these. It's time to claim with that same conviction other things that point to life in God. Even when I'm still a work in progress, I will claim life and not death!

I am healed.

I am healthy.

I can eat wonderful food when I'm very hungry to the glory of God.

I have self-control.

I have patience.

I am worthy.

I am valuable.

I am seen.

I have a purpose.

God delights in me.

I have success.

I am rich.

I am blessed.

I am beloved.

I am cherished.

I have God-given talent.

I am unique and important.

What I have to say is important.

I like these words better. I feel better when I say them. And I am beginning to believe them with each passing day that I say them, whether I feel like it or not! Much of my journey out of the wilderness has had a lot to do with how I speak to myself and others and the thoughts I allow myself to have. I've learned that to meditate the word of God brings peace. To speak the word of God, however, brings revolution to toxic belief systems that hold us back, and ultimate FREEDOM! It's been Thought The Wilderness that I've learned the power of my words. I am kind to myself now most of the time and I see the fruit of begging to believe what God says about me!

After six months of starting Libier.com, with the intention of raising money for Bridget's Dream, I had the beautiful choice to continue my blog just for me. I couldn't have done it without the fire of a higher calling at the beginning. I didn't love myself enough to do what I secretly loved to do just for myself. After Leah's phone call, I began to pray that God would direct my next steps. Nothing was wasted. I believe God was calling me to more healing. There is no point in trying to help the world unless I am first learning how to do it myself, and even then, I am going to make so many mistakes. My motto is: Don't follow me, friend. Walk along side of me so we can learn together! My mess is different from your mess but we are all in some mess. I don't presume to know better than you. I just know different. But let's walk together because it feels so much better to do life with you! God showed me the most heroic thing I could ever do to create lasting change in this world was to be me. But so much of me was buried under the rubble of fear and shame. I had to walk through more fire, more emotional pain, forgive more, heal more, fight with God's Word more. And guess what that produced? More freedom! To know me. To love me. To respect me. To treat myself with dignity. To celebrate me. I worked on myself more than on trying to convince others to change; however, as I learned, I shared on the blog.

I wanted my daughters to see their mother as a woman of faith, fiercely in love with Jesus, and fiercely grateful for my own self. How could I tell them to love and accept themselves if I couldn't? I began blogging with a different intention. It was an experiment of sorts. I was less focused on gaining something and more focused on shedding what had hurt me most: toxic thinking and toxic beliefs. Yes, so much was abuse and trauma, but I had the choice now whether or not to partner with the lies I had believed for so long. I didn't want to remain the same. I had hoped I could change for the better. So I continued to blog. I knew I had to do it in a way that was artistically creative, so I inserted the videos, style posts, beauty tutorials, music writing, dancing, vlogs, and such. Even though parts of it have been absolutely fantastic it has also been amazingly challenging and painful. But I would do it all over again because in trying to help the world, God helped me to see myself more clearly. Little glimmers of me were showing up each time I conquered my fears of failure, rejection, pain, loss one post at a time.

So much transformation has taken place, and I thank God for the opportunity to have shared it with all of those who've come to read. It's been such a gradual change for me that sometimes it's easy to miss, but as I recount all that has taken place within my soul, I am in awe of God and grateful of my resilience to not give up on me. I began to discover talent I never knew I had. It was so exciting to finally be utilizing areas of my brain that had been dormant. I felt challenged and vibrant. So I pressed on in a different direction. In the midst of this new chapter, I got a little stuck. People started noticing me, so I knew I must have been doing something right. But I still wasn't where I wanted to be, so I became upset only a few people were reading. I was reminded to rejoice for what I had and to believe God was growing me as he saw fit. Can you imagine me trying to share with people while my life was still one huge mess? Even now, I know I don't know it all, please take my words and seek God's wisdom as to how to apply them to your life for I am a flawed human. If you want the truth, with love and respect, I suggest you seek the Lord and his Word. That's where I've found my truth. Needless to say, I always ask God to help me lead his people well. He's taught me that good leaders go under their people and lift them up. I know I'm not qualified on my own, but God has called me to share my story and believe in his awesomeness to bring it to the right person at the right time. I was figuring out how to be a blogger and, as my Instagram and blog began to improve and grow more, I wanted to have thousands of more followers, and I began losing sight of who I was following. And why I was where I was. I thought it was up to me to be awesome, and I became obsessed with growth. I began each day asking to be humbled and being grateful for the people who saw my life as an inspiration. I think it becomes so easy to see someone and think he or she has it all together. My hope in life is to show that is not the case, especially with me. My message is this: "With faith, everything is possible for one who believes" (Mark 9:23). Not just some. All! Behind every good-looking photo on my Instagram, there was a very scared little girl wanting to do her best. Wondering if she was good enough.

Through my mess, God remained faithful. He directed me back on the right path. I became more focused on changing from within, for myself. Less on competing with anyone else, more on creating content that delighted me. I took responsibility for my thoughts, actions, and relationships. I parted with my depression, my orphan mentality, and my pessimistic streak (well we're still working on this. Work in progress!). I parted with victim mentality. If I got hurt or experienced pain from healing still, I allowed myself to feel the uncomfortable emotions without distracting from the pain. But I didn't partner with a victim mentality. There's a difference in being a victim of something horrible and falling back into victimization.Self-pity is a slippery slope, so when I grieved, I remembered: "all things God works for the good of those who love him, who have been called according to his purpose" (Romans 8:28). When I was too afraid and didn't want to move forward, I would tell myself. "For me, to live is Christ and to die is gain" (Philippians 1:21). No longer was I pretending to be okay when I truly wasn't. I could finally part with the people pleaser inside of me, or should I say the liar. Can you imagine that I wanted people to like me so much that I lied? I said and did things I didn't want to do for the sake of a person liking me? That's lying to myself and the people I want to impress. I recognized people pleasing wasn't being loving, so I decided to change. I didn't want to live like that. I wanted my no to be a no and my yes to be a yes! I started learning how to speak the truth in love. To lovingly confront people and situations when I felt called to bring a difficult subject into resolution. God gave me the courage to be me, say what I mean, and mean what I say. But do I have this down perfectly? No! I have to choose to be the new me every morning. I notice that, when I slide back, it's so I can go forward even more in the next phase of healing. I've learned to embrace the process I'm in the back-and-forth sort of process. To a recovering perfectionist, this can be so frustrating. We already worked on this, God! Come on. I got a gold star on the last test, why are you making me retake? Ha! I believe God is more interested in who we become through mess than how or if we attain a perfect score and then struggling with pride. Pride is a tricky monster. But nothing God can't overcome. I will never be a "finished" product until I die and go see my beloved Jesus. I will need his loving mercy and grace when I make mistakes until I take my last breath. But this I do know: my eighteen grandchildren will know a new woman in Christ. Amen! Progress over perfection!

They say failure is in the same neighborhood as success. I saw my "failed" attempt at raising money as a learning opportunity that would help me in my next season. I began putting my more balanced energy into creating great content for the people who did read my blog. I did my very best at staying true to myself. I messed up a lot but I learned a lot. Through these couple years of blogging, I developed a heart for encouraging women to feel and look their best, as is. Today, right this second. Not when they get richer and can afford new, more labeled clothing. Not when they lost thirty pounds. Not when they got Botox and they looked younger. Now, as is. I could understand so deeply what someone went through in all the phases of not liking themselves. So I began seeing myself in each woman. I loved when someone would reach out to me and say God used what I wrote to help them that day. The best part of blogging!

I knew I wasn't where I used to be, but I still had a long way to go. I wanted to smoosh all my passions together. Performing arts, style, beauty, brains. And my blog became something I never thought possible. I started being asked to come on TV to do style segments with Karina Banda on Univision, the Spanish channel. Then God miraculously opened a door for me at KCRA with Lisa Gonzales. Then I got more TV opportunities than I could have ever imagined. Almost any time I was about to go on live, I would be on my knees in the bathroom of the TV stations, praying for God to help me. I've spoken at elementary schools about my life. I've been flown to New York to style former supermodel Kim Alexis for the cover of Eloquent Magazine. I've had the privilege of working with brands I loved growing up with—and all because I said yes to an adventure with God. It has not been easy. But it's been possible because God is bigger than our dreams. Bigger than our failures. Bigger than our problems. Bigger than our fears.

He has taken a scared, wounded, low self-esteem little Mexican girl and loved her back to life and into womanhood that feels so empowering. He has given me my life back tenfold. When he promised me in the Wilderness that he would pay me double in joy what I'd endured in pain, I believed him at his Word. He has not disappointed me! And he continues to lavishly give me riches that cannot fade: joy, contentment, and peace. He gives me the honor and privilege to speak to you. That's him paying me back. To be able to be in your hands right now, speaking into your life, is something I would have never dreamed about. He "is able to do immeasurably more than all we ask or imagine, according to his power that is at work within us" (Ephesians 3:20). If he can do it for me, he can do it for you. Don't lose heart in anything, darling. Don't give up. Claim what is yours! The freedom that lies within you is fierce, and God has faith in you. We need you to be you. God won't let you down. Like a loving father, he'll light your way, step by step. You can trust in him!

Now I sit at the end of this chapter of my life knowing there still is much to improve but in awe of the glory of God upon my life. The newfound love for myself and the acceptance of what was—the excitement of what's to come and the hope for how God will turn my ashes into beauty, even more than I already have witnessed. My soul is at rest in a new and profound way I have never experienced before. No longer do I feel the need to hurt me. No longer do I feel the need to say sorry every two seconds of my life. I am not sorry for who I am or for being in a room. I am a beloved child of God, and I was made in his image to reflect his glory. I no longer feel bad about my strengths or beat myself up over my weaknesses. There is compassion within me, like honey dripping down into the deepest parts of my soul. My goal is to swim in the grace of God daily and receive his unexplainable gift of mercy often. I find myself getting closer and closer to being all that God's love designed me to be. The very essence of who I am feels light and free rather than dark, lonely, and damaged. I feel healthy in spirit and in truth. I delight in freedom to choose to be myself. All of me, all of the time. It's a great feeling. Unconditional love for my human self. Ah, what a thought! I don't have to be perfect to love myself. I can look at myself in the mirror and say words that affirm who God tells me I am, and with each passing day, I find myself truly believing them. I have forgiven my past and allowed God to pull up the roots of bitterness and anger that consumed me. I finally believe I am worthy of God's love because of his sacrifice for me. I can finally, graciously, and joyfully receive the gift of his life in exchange for mine.

As an adult, I had the choice to stay in a victim mentality or push past the pain of healing through to a victorious and purposeful life in Christ. I drew strength from my husband and I saw myself in my little girls. He used the love for my husband and daughters to fuel a passion for changing from within so I would not move forward with my habitual sin. You see, my girls will grow up and do as I do, not as I said. I have come to terms with the fact that I will never be a perfect human, much less a perfect wife or parent. So I know that I will fail my family time and time again. There is a difference, though, in choosing to remain in the same sin for the sake of not "going there." For the sake of not enduring hardship and pain. I would go through the pain of healing one million times more if it meant for me to not infect my children with the generational sin. We are stronger than we think, you know. There is power in weakness and falling apart at the feet of Jesus. For then and only then he can rebuild us miraculously.

Thank you, Jesus, for everything you've done for this little Mexican girl. You traded your life so I could have life and live it abundantly! It felt so uncomfortable to receive you for so long, but we did it! All those years of going to church and hearing pastor Louis talk about how to receive Christ now was making sense! I feel truly loved and truly known by God, and that enables me and encourages me to push forward each day even through the many trials I still face. In no way has my life become easier. In some ways, I believe the battle has raised to new levels. But so has my faith and my understanding of who I am in God. So I fight the good fight. I sit in silence and pray that my journey will help anyone who is still having trouble receiving all you have for him or her, Jesus. Thank you for never giving up on us. For having faith in us and believing we can fight for our lives and believe you at your Word. Even in moments of complete despair, you never give up on us. We praise you for your name is beautiful, Jesus.

You have won my heart. Take it; seal it! I came to know the savior of my soul. I was so skeptical of Jesus Christ of Nazareth, but his passion for my soul and my healing overpowered the greatest and deepest wounds in me. His love surged in like an avalanche

I am still broken. I still have issues. However, now I have something so precious, which has made me a new person. I have something so precious that nothing listed above could take away from me, and that is the love of Christ. My dignity is in him and him alone. I was not defiled by what happened to me; I defiled myself when I didn't know how to process the trauma, and I started making bad choices based on my hurt. Joyce Meyer said it best, "Hurt people, hurt." I was mainly hurting myself. Self-hatred and all. But hurt people can rest in the hands of Jesus and be restored to better much better than they were!

I humbly share with you my life, that you might gain insight from my brokenness. May God bless you and keep you. Thank you for reading.

If it were up to me, this is what the cover would've looked like!

Thank God for Sammy and Hayley!

THROUGH THE *Wilderness*

by libie

A LOVE LETTER

Here's a letter I wrote to myself after writing the first draft of this book. I'd say God accomplished his work.

Libier,

I am sitting here, writing this book God called you to write before you were even born. He knew every twist and turn that would catapult you into your destiny. He knew how much you'd learn, and that in spite of all the pain you went through, you still chose him. You chose to enter into his healing even when enduring the pain soberly. You came close to ending your life because of the pain you felt, but he held you together. You chose to walk through the fire because you wanted so badly to believe that there had to be a better life than what you had experienced. The life you lived before didn't have God at the center, and now you have hope that will never cease. You chose to wake up, day in and day out, while he nursed you back to health. You chose to put one foot in front of the other, even when the pain got so deep that you physically felt ill from the way your soul ached.

I sit here in awe of how brave you've been and, most importantly, in awe of what God has done through you, for you, and with you. I will celebrate with you right now because I know no one will ever truly understand what you've been through aside from God; it's no one's place to understand you like that, so we will not put that expectation or responsibility on others. But I see you, I celebrate you, and I love you so very much. I will take care of you from now on. I will a choose different lifestyle now. I will do things out of loving and respecting you, and I will try not to harm you. Your willingness to help people in your pain and suffering have allowed God to create in you an empathetic and compassionate heart. You love those around you the best way you know how. You wish freedom and healing for everyone you meet. You chose to speak the truth in love. You know they have a story too. You understand their hearts hurts too and that they too are deeply terrified in some way, that they don't have what it takes for this life, or that they aren't worthy of love or the call they suspect God has for them.

You believe everyone's pain matters, no matter the story behind it, not one is more powerful than the other. You believe God wants nothing more than to heal us all uniquely and individually. You stand with people in unity and truly believe the best in everyone you see. I see that about you, and it delights me to know that I am you. You've done a fantastic job, little girl. You have never given up, in spite of the gut-wrenching pain you've endured. Your faith is ever growing because you believe Jesus, that he is the author and the perfecter of it, and you know that, and cling to that freedom. I have seen how you've forgiven those who've abused you in unspeakable ways. I've seen you love the people who abused you as you hurt from what they'd done to you. I've seen you pray for those who treated you wrong and bless them even as you were healing from them. I've seen you ministering to the hearts of those who hurt you telling them of the love of Jesus and sharing with them why you are choosing to forgive all they've done to you. I have seen you lay your life down for your friends and your enemies. I have seen you take the road least traveled, and for that, I thank you. You, my darling, are fierce and faithful. I have seen you change so that your husband and your children could enjoy the best version of you. So you could enjoy the best version of you.

You believed God had better for you and your family, and you persevered through the painful change. In your time of healing, you did so many wrong things. You hurt those who love you, in many ways, but you've swam in the grace that God has given you and hoped and prayed that God's grace would cover your multitude of sins. You've asked for forgiveness and accepted it for yourself. You know full well that you are loved not by what you do but because of whose you are. You did the best you could with the circumstances you had. The most important thing, baby girl, is that you always look unto Jesus, and you never gave up. You have changed a pattern of toxic thinking, and you've put away your old self, sometimes on an hourly basis, to trade in for the riches the Lord has promised you. The richness of living in community with him all the days of your life. You have become rich. Rich in love that was covered by the lies of the enemy and the love you thought you would never be able to be worthy of.

You have become a prayer warrior, and that is the biggest asset you have to your name. You have seen miracle after miracle in your life and in the lives of people around you because of your willingness to look foolish in front of men and believe, with all your might, in your faithful, mighty, and powerful God. You have come to love him with all of your heart! Your life's purpose is to be in communion and completely tethered to Jesus. You've come to believe that safety is not where you're safe; it's in the presence of the almighty who makes all your fears go away. His perfect love has cast out all your fear, and he has made you new. You're walking into your promised land right now because of the faith you have in God. He has made you whole and content with your life right now, and the peace that surpasses all your understanding guards your mind and heart in Christ. There is nothing he can't do. You believe this now.

Never has the walk been perfect. You've failed along the way. But my dear, he has never failed you. Your whole life reflects a good, amazing heavenly Father. Your life reflects the glory of his power, and there is no shame in being a reflection of who he is. All that you are is due to all God is. You know you're not better or worse than anyone else, and you love to encourage others to find that freedom within. You truly want all people to know this love. This peace. This unending joy. You especially see little girls of all ages being called into dignity. Boys who have healed from their abuse made whole! I know the desire deep within your heart to see a generation of men and women healed from sexual immorality, ceasing the objectification of women, to heal from the broken places that rob our lives in ways we can't even comprehend. I know you have a dream to see those who struggle with abuse, addiction, and self-hatred to finally see their hearts' true desires are to be truly known and fully loved, and that can be solved by one name, Jesus Christ!

I know you feel as though you don't know much, and you might not. But this is your testimony—what you've been through—and although you won't ever have all the answers about God or life, you have the proof of who

Jesus is for you: the savior of your soul, the reason why you live. So let's celebrate the journey through the Wilderness, for here that chapter ends! On to your land of milk and honey.

Love,

Libier

If this book had an impact in your life and you'd like to share for a chance

to be featured on the blog, email us at:

LibierFreedom@gmail.com

84572408R00112

Made in the USA
Lexington, KY
23 March 2018